Florence, Dante and Me

A Canadian Student Goes Italian
For a Year, 1960-61

Buon Viaggio, Serena! Robert Thomson

Robert Stuart Thomson

GODWIN BOOKS
2017

May 15/2018

Published by Godwin Books, Victoria, B.C.

GODWIN BOOKS

www.godwinbooks.com

Library and Archives Canada Cataloguing in Publication

ISBN: 978-0-9958760-0-2

Cover design by Iryna Spica
Typeset in *Plantin* with *Italian Old Style* display at
SpicaBookDesign

Printed in Canada

Introduction

THE SOURCES OF THIS BOOK
AND HOW IT CAME TO BE

The material in this book comes from a bundle of about fifty letters written in 1960-61 when I was studying in Florence thanks to a scholarship from the Italian government. The letters were written to my fiancée who stayed in Vancouver to pursue her studies at UBC (the University of British Columbia). During the first few months in Italy I missed her badly and tried to persuade her to join me. To my chagrin these efforts were in vain. Nevertheless I kept sending her detailed letters of my life in Italy. My purpose was to keep the flame of love alive; it was also to record my experiences and reflect on them. I returned to Vancouver to discover that she had found a new love but that's another story and not mine for the telling. I respect her privacy and won't give her name; I have also omitted all passages of a very private nature.

Around November of 1960 my fiancée got the bright idea of culling highlights from my letters, typing them up, and circulating them among friends and professors with whom we had studied. Dr. Grant, the professor of Latin whom I write fondly about in my letters was one of them. Dr. Rachel Giese of the Italian department was another. When I realized who was reading my letters I took extra care with them. According to my fiancée they enjoyed reading of my adventures. This got me thinking: Hmm, maybe one day, with lots of revision, they could be made into a book. I could even add photos to make it more interesting.

Many years passed by. I got involved in my career. I took early retirement (1995) and started a new career as a writer and publisher. I wrote *Great songs for the English Classroom, Hot tips for real estate investors, Italian for the Opera, Operatic Italian* and *Love songs in Spanish for Enjoyment and learning.* I also published two books by my great-uncle, George Godwin (1889-1974): *The Eternal Forest* and *Why stay we here?* (a memoir about World War I).The next book on my agenda was this one on my year in Italy. I would have been astounded if anyone in 1960-1 had told me that I would publish it in 2017, fifty-six years later.

As for the graphics in this book, I am glad that I kept photos of most of the people I got to know in Italy. You will find them throughout the book. I have also included photos to illustrate many of the things that impressed me: cities, buildings, paintings, sculpture, movies, books and landscapes. Many of the photos I have taken from a handsome tome called *Il Paesaggio italico nella Divina Commedia* (Italian Landscape in the Divine Comedy). Written about 1910, its stark black and white photos reflect well the old Italy that I was getting to know in 1960-1.

Several things in this book were added in 2017: most of the photos, some comments in the text (these have been highlighted with brackets) and the copious footnotes. The footnotes often contain lengthy reflections on issues raised in the original letters.

MY FAMILY OF ORIGIN AND FIRST
TWO YEARS OF COLLEGE

I was born in Vancouver on April 30, 1940. My ancestors were a mixture of Anglo-Saxon and Celtic My parents were average Canadians of British background. My stepfather worked in a local office of the Federal treasury department; my mother was a housewife. Neither had gone to university. I think my mother inherited a rich DNA through her father's family, the Godwins. There is a strong current of innovative thinking in that family, as I discovered when I began reprinting my great-uncle George Godwin's books in 1994.

I don't know quite how to account for my interest in Italian opera and the French and Italian languages. It probably started in 1951 when I saw Mario Lanza play Caruso in the movie, *The Great Caruso*. I was converted in a flash. This interest was encouraged by my grandmother who bought me some recordings by Caruso. I thought it was quite wonderful that she had actually heard him sing around 1910 in the old Vancouver opera house. For grades one to twelve I attended various schools in North and West Vancouver. I was not much interested in studying until about grade ten when I changed my attitude. By grade twelve I was doing well, winning the general proficiency award in academics in grades eleven and twelve at West Van High.

During my first year at UBC I continued with French but also took introductory courses in Latin, Italian and German. I became very familiar with flashcards. It was in the Latin class that I met the young lady to whom I wrote from Italy. Second year at UBC went well. I was accepted into an honors program in French and Italian. UBC was very elitist in that era and encouraged outstanding students to sign up for an honors program which demanded extra courses and high marks. The highlight of the program came in fourth year when one took an Oxford style year-long private tutorial with one of the best professors in the department and wrote a fifty page paper (in French) under his direction. It was more or less a given that you would be going on to a PhD. But I am getting ahead of myself. Let me tell you more about my second year at UBC because it prepared me for Italy in several ways.

My second year was an exciting intellectual adventure. I had several outstanding teachers. They inspired me to work hard and get the grades that would qualify me for a third year scholarship. Latin was taught by Dr. Leonard Grant, a native Scot who taught not just Latin but also many fascinating things about life in ancient Rome. Genevieve Bird was a Parisian who taught a seminar for honors students on dictées and translations. Dr. Kurt Weinberg (from Yale) spoke French like a native and brilliantly glossed extracts from French literature. Dr. Rachel Giese taught the second year course in Italian and advised me to skip her classes and read Dante and Manzoni on my own. It was Rachel who suggested that I apply for an all expenses paid year in Italy sponsored by the Italian government.

I applied for two year long scholarships for third year and won both of them: one to Italy and the other (sponsored by the Canadian University Students Organization) to any Canadian university of my choice. Both scholarships would cover travel, tuition, and a monthly allowance for the academic year. Which should I choose? Italy (Perugia and Florence) or Canada (Laval University in Quebec City)? Laval was 95% French speaking and would be a good place to study French. But Italy! That was a dream come true and I didn't anguish over the decision. Where in Italy? Rome and Florence were on my short list but I chose Florence because I was dazzled by the long list of great artists and writers from that city: Giotto, Petrarca, Boccaccio, Brunelleschi, Botticelli, Machiavelli, Michelangelo, Leonardo da Vinci, Galileo. The list seemed endless but the one who intrigued me the most was Dante Alighieri.

The terms of this Italian scholarship were liberal. There were no restrictions as to where you lived or what you studied. Taking final exams was optional. My plan was to take the train to Quebec City and spend a week there (I wanted to see what I was going to miss by choosing Italy) before taking a ship to Scotland and making my way down to Italy (with a two day stop in London).

VANCOUVER AND UBC IN 1958-1960

In many ways Vancouver was a rather dull and materialistic place in the period 1958-1962 but there were enticing currents of Romanticism in the air. Italian songs were often playing on the radio. They were glamorous and exotic and it was hard not to dream a little of Italy when listening to them. Domenico Modugno's *Volare,* Dean Martin's *That's Amore!,* Frank Sinatra's *Vicino al Mare* (also known as *I have but one love)* Rosemary Clooney's *Mambo Italiano* and Julius La Rosa's *Eh, Cumpari!* are typical. Movies about Italy were also alluring and sparked interest: *Roman Affair, Roman Holiday, Three Coins in a Fountain*. There were several. Perhaps the most intriguing aspect of these movies is how Italians were portrayed: good-looking, smartly dressed, proud, passionate, imaginative, charming wooers, sensitive to other people. Many of my generation were enchanted by the beauty and glamor of Italy, not to mention her distinctive style that could be seen even in everyday things such as Vespa scooters, Olivetti typewriters and "Vesuvius" espresso coffee machines. Italy had panache and style.

Vancouver had some culture (in the European sense) but compared with Italy it didn't amount to much at all. There was one opera company, The Vancouver Opera, but it produced only three or four operas a year. There was a city art gallery but its holdings in Italian Renaissance art were negligible. There was only one good bookstore in town, Bill Duthie's on Robson St., and probably only one good shop for buying long playing classical records, Len Timbers', also on Robson. It was a very different world from today: No walkmans, message minding machines, CDs, DVDs, computers, cell phones, etc. Long distance telephone calls were ruinously expensive. Probably the richest part of the cultural scene was movies. Some of the best ones that I recall seeing were *War and Peace, My Fair Lady, South Pacific, Twelve Angry Men, Spartacus* and *Ben Hur. Spartacus* and *Ben Hur* were powerful and historically pretty accurate. Such movies would help me to piece together ancient Rome when I went to Italy.

The University of British Columbia provided some glamor and exoticism. A small theater ("The Old Auditorium") gave free noon hour concerts of a very high caliber. I remember seeing the Red Army Chorus, Jose Greco (the famous flamenco dancer), Andres Segovia and Pete Seeger, to name but a few. I also have fond recollections of a very suave, witty English ballroom dance teacher, Mr. Vincent (always in a tux, even for his 8 a.m. dance class) who enriched the lives of those of us who chose his course in ballroom dancing to fill the university's physical education requirement. There was nothing staid about the rumba or the tango.

In the Faculty of Arts it was hip to be interested in Europe and to study European history and European languages. Such study whetted one's appetite for Europe and many students travelled there as soon as they could. Some even went so far as to assume a new identity. I realize now that to some degree this is what I was doing: becoming as Italian as possible.

THE RATIONALE FOR THIS BOOK

I will feel very gratified if this book inspires some people to take the trouble to learn the language of the country they travel to. Such knowledge will bring understanding of the culture and enable them to connect with people in a more meaningful way. To study another language is a huge compliment to the native speakers of that language.

I urge high school seniors to give serious thought to majoring in a foreign language. The benefits of doing this are not always obvious but I hope that reading this book will show how knowledge of a second language opens many doors.

Spending one's junior year abroad has become common practice and there are many colleges that offer good programs. This is a very good thing. Living abroad for a year greatly enriches one's life. It's also a challenge and a test of one's adaptability. It is not always easy: there are language skills to hone, new friends to reach out to and a new culture to explore. One has to become aware of cultural differences and make allowances for them. I did some things right and other things not so right, as you will see in the following pages. I hope what I write about them will prove to be helpful.

One of the unexpected benefits of my year in Italy was to see my life in a more moral and spiritual way. I gained insights into my upbringing and education and began to see that they had molded me in a very narrow way. I was somewhat like Dante, lost in a dark wood, a *selva oscura*. I hope my remarks on this subject will resonate with some readers.

Table of Contents

1961

This well-travelled map covers the cities I visited.
Mantua is not on the map. It lies between Bologna and Verona

Robert Thomson at the Canadian National Railway station,
July 20, 1960

July 25, 1960   Vancouver

I finished the second year of university in April, 1960. From May to July I worked as a laborer helping to construct the North Vancouver Recreation Center. I am now ready for my great adventure: a year in Italy. When I arrive at the Canadian National Railway station on Main Street in Vancouver a pleasant surprise awaits me. A friend, Carol Itter, had phoned *The Sun* newspaper and suggested that they send someone down to the station to interview me and take a photo for the newspaper. As I told the reporter, my plan was to take the train to Quebec City (and look over the French Department at Laval University), travel by ship to Scotland, hitchhike to London (where I would stay a few days) then set off for Italy (Perugia) by train. Then my Italian adventure would really begin.

Laval University:
the old campus in the Haute Ville (Upper town)

July 30, 1960   Quebec City

Dearest J,

I like Laval University—learned, friendly professors and a real cloister atmosphere. In the music faculty you can hear Gregorian chants and when you look out a window there it is below you: the mighty St. Lawrence flowing ever eastward. I can just imagine Wolfe's ships coming up the river. I saw the new science buildings on the western edge of town and was amazed at the speed of construction. Since the new Liberal provincial government got in, federal government aid is no longer being refused. Can you imagine that reactionary dictator Duplessis refusing to accept federal aid for so many years! What an ass! Everyone suffered because of his gigantic ego. So many years of stagnation!

The 'quartier latin' is intriguing. Narrow streets labyrinthing the side of a hill, somber convents of faded red brick, church bells ringing and nuns and priests sedately walking to vespers. This city is still in the seventeenth century. Although I had heard what it was like I never would have believed it without seeing for myself. My first impression was that people in the streets were putting on an act. Surely they could speak English! Why were they clinging so stubbornly to the old ways? I guess you'd have to spend years here to figure it out. People speak a strange, harsh kind of French which I find hard to understand. I feel like a complete idiot because I have studied French for six years now. **[1]**

I have a room in the house of Mme. Cloutier, right across the street from the old university. I see little kids playing in the street, workers digging up the road, hoods in cafés, and beautiful girls in the street, all in high heels, billowy, gingham-type dresses and long hair swept up in fashionable style. All are speaking French.

I dropped in on Professor Garneau. (I think he's the "recteur" i.e. more or less the dean.) and introduced myself. I told him that I had received two scholarships for the coming year, one for Italy (a scholarship offered by the *Ministero degli affari esteri*) and the other for any Canadian University I choose (it's offered by the CUS, the Union of Canadian University Students). I explained to Monsieur Garneau that it was a difficult choice because I have always been interested in the history of French-Canada and the French language but Florence with its rich Renaissance history was hard to refuse. He was very nice about it, said he understood and even granted me permission to audit some courses before I set sail for Italy. So here I am, spending at least five hours a day auditing courses at Laval University, getting a taste of what I am going to miss. Jeanne Lapointe's course on Racine is very good and so is Dumouchel's course on the Renaissance. The course on Baudelaire had only a few people in it. I got into a chat with one of them. **[2]**

I can't decide whether to fly to Europe from Montreal ($215.) or take a ship for $225. I decide to sail.

August 7, 1960   London, England

My dearest J,

The voyage across the Atlantic on the *Ivernia* could easily have turned out tiring and boring. I got the wrong ship: a religious convention of 800 people! This did not seem to promise a good time. Fortunately I found a lively Scottish group and every night we sang and drank until the wee hours. The ship landed at Greenock, Scotland. From there I hitched my way to London. It took four rides. The fourth ride I got near Gretna Greene with a Cockney named "Blackie". He was a friendly fellow, full of stories about his life. He was also generous and insisted on paying for the fish and chips.

In London I stayed with my stepfather's sister, Agnes, and her husband Jack, from Victoria, British Columbia. Their son John is studying painting here and their daughter Jan is also living here. She very recently got hitched to Ian McDougall, a fine jazz trombone player. Ian has found a job playing in Jack Dankworth's big band, one of the best in England. I helped them move a huge piano into their apartment. I visited The National Gallery and one of the paintings which really impressed me was Leonardo Da Vinci's *Virgin of the Rocks*. This is the first Italian Renaissance painting I have ever seen. I can't wait to see more. I also saw a good movie of *The Marriage of Figaro* (the play, not the opera) at the new National Film Center on the south bank of the Thames.

Florence, Dante and Me

August 11, 1960   Perugia

Dearest J,

I am off! I took the train to Dover then a small ship to France.
The crossing was exciting: the English Channel and the cliffs
of France just ahead! The sea was blue, a real blue and it
was a bright sunny day. I am really wound up about what's
in store for me! On the ship I treated myself to a full meal,
with wine. For me, this was splurging. On my $100 a month
stipend I won't be doing it often (although as a reserve I do
have $600. saved from my summer job). Then I took the train
to Perugia in Umbria. Just before arriving in Perugia I saw
Lake Trasimeno, which is very marshy. I have learned that it
was here in the Punic Wars that Hannibal and his elephants
drove the Roman soldiers into the lake where they drowned.
I wonder if it has lots of armor and weapons on the bottom.
    Perugia. How strange it is again, like in Quebec City,
to walk down narrow, winding streets. *Via del Cane!* (The
Street of the Dog!). On the corner of a building is a horrid
griffin with bloodied, mocking jowls. *Cave cane!* Swine!
Cur! *Via di qua!* (Get out!) The heat is oppressive and like
nothing I have ever experienced. In the air you can hear
a great chorus of cicadas clicking away. The buildings are
three-storied and on the balconies there are flower pots
and pettycoats hanging from clotheslines. I see brick buildings rotting with age. The iron grills on their windows look
forbidding. I glance into a doorway: an old man, yellow

and bent with age, is sawing planks with a saw that looks medieval. They work hard, these Italians, and I admire them for it. The waitress at the Jamaica (a restaurant where I have started going regularly) has to serve eight tables. I think that's too much to handle yet she is always cheerful.

Mysterious Etruscan Perugia

I guess Perugia shouldn't exist (or there shouldn't be much left of it). It luckily escaped bombing during the last war but only because after taking Rome the Allies made a very fast thrust north and bypassed Perugia. Florence and the region north of here took the pounding instead. Geoffrey, a young Oxford grad in history, told me this (I must acknowledge sources!) and much more, last night, over supper at the Jamaica. There was a full moon and we went for a walk after dinner. I really got a tour and much interesting information. He said that Perugia was built before Romulus founded Rome. It was an Etruscan center and this explains the huge triumphal arch in the center of the city. It's monumental and perfectly preserved. I could gaze at it for hours. You have to wonder at the things it's witnessed and the amazing number of years it has been there. *Chi furono, questi Etruschi?* (Who were they, these Etruscans?)

Etruscan wall and arch in Perugia

There are about one hundred forty churches in Perugia (one serves as a major museum) and a medieval fortress. From the top of this fortress (two hundred feet up) you get an amazing panorama of the surrounding countryside. You can see Assisi, only twenty miles away, glimmering through the warm summer air. I am eager to see the city of Saint Francis. There are always lovely breezes coming from the south-west, up the Tiber and over to us.

Assisi as seen from the south

Most people here get up early and then sleep for a few hours in the afternoon. After the nap everyone dresses to the nines and saunters on up to the wide Corso Vannucci where the stores, open air market and outdoor wine and coffee shops are open until nine. Everyone in town walks up and down the Corso, which is closed to automobile traffic. It is not uncommon to see men walking arm in arm and it is common for men to wear their jacket over their shoulders like a cloak. People walk *adagio* up and down the Corso, observing, smiling, greeting, nodding, ogling. The game is to look sophisticated and *fare una bella figura* (which means to look good and appear contented with yourself). Everyone plays it well. **[3]**

Florence, Dante and Me

Il Corso Vannucci

I am enjoying the pace of life here. It's pretty easy-going. The Italians call it *dolce far niente* ("sweet doing nothing"). Dressing well is important. The men dress a bit flashily but they definitely have flair: white leather shoes or suedes with pointed toes. Fruity, by Canadian standards. Their dress shirts have much broader collars than ours and I think they look better. The tight pants are quite splendid for showing off a well-turned leg. The women dress to please: high heels almost all the time, billowy, dainty, feminine dresses that show a little of the knee, and their hair is swept up in an elegant style. Their posture, bearing and figure are quite striking. The old saying probably applies here: *Per essere bella bisogna soffrire.* (To be beautiful you have to suffer.)

I went into a tobacco shop for some stamps the other day and serving behind the counter was a beautiful, majestic young woman with expressive eyes—a real Sophia

Loren type. She just stared at me with her enormous dark eyes for what seemed the longest time, then finally said, *"Dica!"* (i. e. "Say! Say something! Speak, you Moron!"). I had been too stunned to speak and mumbled away as I ordered a few stamps. What an anticlimax! I find some of these little exchanges so interesting, dramatic and somehow loaded. These Italians really look at you square in the eye; they're not like Canadians. I have learned that apart from post offices the only places allowed to sell postage stamps are the tobacconists and this stems from an edict by Napoleon.

Night life for Italians consists in going to the local bar, drinking wine, and watching television. Many American programs are shown here with dubbed in Italian. The same goes for movies. Water is scarce and is carried and hoarded in pop bottles. Wine (the local variety) can be bought for as little as 25 cents a bottle; a pack of cigarettes, 20 cents; a three course meal (all you can eat!) and a quarter liter of wine for 55 cents. Here's what I had last night at the Jamaica restaurant: a huge plate of spaghetti *bolognese,* then a steak, then a tomato and lettuce salad. To top it off, fruit for dessert. This was all washed down by half a liter of red wine. Total bill: 75 cents. Not bad, eh? Okay, it's a cheap restaurant, but can you beat it?

About the water: there's no hot running water here and you can't even get cold running water between noon and midnight. Apparently the water is run in via an old Roman aqueduct.

On weekends excursions are organized at reasonable rates by the *Università per Stranieri* (Foreigners).

Unfortunately, this week I put off buying a ticket too long and missed a Sunday trip to the beach at Senigallia on the Adriatic, plus an art tour to a few out-of-the-way Umbrian towns.

I had lunch today with Hassan from the Sudan and James from Malta. Pretty cosmopolitan, eh? I find I have much in common with the students I have been meeting. We are all here to learn Italian and enjoy Italy This afternoon I heard a lecture on Signorelli, a fifteenth century painter, given by the great professor Mariani of the University of Naples. I can honestly say that he is the best (the most flamboyant, anyway) lecturer I have ever heard: impeccably dressed, and so voluble and expressive. And the gestures! A chop of the hand to emphasize a point, a snap of the fingers to signal a change in the slides. What style! Fantastic! Inexpressible! The lectures are held in an elegant palace: Il Palazzo Gallenga. It dates from the mid-1700s and is quite grand, with gold chandeliers.

Il Palazzo Gallenga (Università per Stranieri)

I dropped in on another lecture at random. The professor was teaching economics with maps, graphs, pictures, etc. He was talking nostalgically about "autarchia", which is the economic principle of a country becoming totally self-sufficient economically. I read somewhere that this was one of Mussolini's goals for Italy. This professor had a sad look about him. I think he is still a great admirer of *Il Duce*.

A typical classroom in Il Palazzo Gallenga

Yesterday I went on a bus trip organized by the University. The destination was Urbino (forty miles north-east of here, in the Apennines) then Pesaro on the Adriatic. I made several friends (and some enemies) by projecting my bass-baritone voice and anxious personality to everyone within earshot of the rear of the bus. The Yugoslavs sitting next to me loved it; the French behind me hated it. By and large the group on the bus was either very shy, dull, quiet or something which I can't define.

Florence, Dante and Me

The Ducal Palace, Urbino

Urbino is a lovely medieval town. The grand ducal palace is worth seeing. Walking down the corridors of the palace I had the impression I was back in the fourteenth century. It is wonderfully preserved, even the furniture. From numerous little balconies and alcoves you get a fine view of the countryside of the *Marche* province. Urbino is famous as the birthplace of Raphael and I saw some of his paintings. In town I saw a quotation chiseled in marble high up on the side of a building (Italy has many of these to honor the great from past centuries.) It was a quote from Michel de Montaigne—and went something like this: *Urbine, où il y a partout à monter et à descendre; le marché y était parce qu'il était samedi.* The subtle fox! I love him. It gave me a funny feeling to think that Montaigne had walked these same streets way back in the 1500's. We studied his essay on friendship in Kurt Weinberg's class last year at UBC.

From Urbino we drove to the beach at Pesaro, about twenty miles to the east. We encountered the Adriatic, 'Hadrian's Sea', and miles and miles of white sand stretching north and south.

I realize now how narrow Italy is. Nowhere is the sea far off. I had lunch with a Yugoslavian couple on the terrace of a restaurant. We had cheese, bread and some kind of raw bacon which I discovered is called *prosciutto crudo*. I supplied the wine: forty-five cents for a large bottle of fairly good stuff. Hard to beat, eh? [Back in Perugia] I have to sign off. I am going down to the hospital to visit a very sick girl from Vancouver: Jan Elderkin, who also goes to UBC. She has taken a year out to travel all over the world and caught some nasty bug in India. I am taking her some oranges and a copy of *For Whom the Bell Tolls*.

August 18, 1960   Perugia

Dear J,

I am sitting at my desk reading Dante in the late afternoon.
All of a sudden, quite unexpectedly, the nearby church
bells start to toll. Beautiful! Ah, the delights of reading!

I went to the *Circolo* (a club for students) this morning. It's a huge student lounge at the *Università per Stranieri.*
You can buy lunch in the cafeteria for eighty cents (500
lire): pasta, salad, bread, and one quarter of a liter of wine.
Amazing! *Everyone* has wine with their meal. It's a given.

A large slug of vermouth costs eight cents. I chatted
with a couple of guys from Kenya, a fellow from Malta, an
Egyptian who is a whiz at billiards and a girl from Frankfurt.
As you can see, it's a cosmopolitan place. The afternoon was
as hot as blazes (I have never felt such heat.) so I went for a
swim in an outdoor pool. Swimming caps are mandatory
so I had to buy one. I am leaving for Rome tomorrow with
Harry, a bearded, eccentric (he wears a black cape everywhere), and very intelligent Greek. We plan to take in a few
events at the Olympic Games if we can get tickets.

Perugia has lots to offer: ancient architecture, an excellent museum of Etruscology and a gallery full of Peruginos,
Lorenzo da Lorenzos, etc. I really like Perugino, especially
his detailed portraits of people. There is such pride in the
faces. I hear that he was Raphael's teacher. That alone says
a lot for him. Perugia also has a music society although it

seems limited to chamber music. I'm planning on taking voice lessons during my year over here but it will have to wait until I have settled in Florence. I think I am a bass-baritone. This is something I've always wanted to do.

Last night I went to a party in a house on a hill here in the city. Below us I could see a meadow enclosed by an ancient wall and in the distance the eerie outline of a castle. The weather was balmy and warm with a sky full of stars in a way that I have never seen before. There were red shooting stars as well. The Milky Way as seen from Italy really is a white ribbon. An American negro with a beautiful baritone voice sang several songs for us: *Summertime, Laura, The St. Louis Blues*. It was very special. He is quite good enough for Broadway!

I have been going to lectures on Italian opera twice a week at the University and have been studying Verdi librettos in my room. These two activities go well together. The lecturer is lively and illustrates his talk with extracts on the gramophone. I have been studying Italian five or six hours a day and I just wish I had more time to watch the Olympics on TV. I did see the finals of the one hundred meter hurdles and saw the Americans clean up: 1st, 2nd and 3rd places.

I have heard from home that my 1949 Studebaker was sold for $200. It was an incredible oil-guzzler and I had to put a quart of oil in it every few days but it was a reliable jalopy and I am sad to see it go.

I forgot to mention John, a guy from Cambridge University who has shown me around town and explained the historical significance of many buildings. He is a whiz at history. We had a going-away party for him a few nights ago in a beautiful ancient house. John epitomizes how good the British system of education can be (if you manage to pass the rigorous exam that everyone takes at age eleven: "the eleven plus"). Before going to university he had had nine years of Latin, seven years of Greek, and had read most of Shakespeare. It's impossible to compete with that! A group of us—John, myself, a girl philosophy grad from Dublin, and an Indian prince (or something!) left the rock and roll group, took a few gallons of wine and went to an obscure corner to talk and recite poetry. John recited Shakespeare and Wilfred Owen beautifully in his soft, sonorous English public school accent. Yours truly did some French Romantics (Nerval, Baudelaire) and Ronnie, the Indian, recited the most melodious, poignant-sounding Indian and Sanskrit verse.

The other day, while winding my way up the dusty, narrow, urchin-running, padrona-yelling Corso Bersaglieri I heard a rollicking harmonica duet played by two little old ragged Italian men. They were bald and poor but happy nonetheless. One played the melody on a Hohner, the other played a bass accompaniment. I sat and listened, then applauded vigorously and gave them a few coins. I went away feeling very happy. I thought that this is typical of the Italian *joie de vivre*. Even though these little guys are earning only a pittance, they still get great pleasure from music, companionship, and whatever other worthwhile and pleasing things life has to offer them.

My spoken Italian is improving only slightly. To improve I really should avoid English-speaking people. Speaking for myself, I think we English speakers feel quite awkward and self-conscious when speaking to each other in a foreign language so I think I will make a point of seeking out Italians and speaking only Italian with them. I will have to be careful that following this rule does not isolate me. **[4]**

Signora Bianchi on her balcony in Perugia

I have found a comfortable room with the Bianchi family. I have a cheerful, bright room on the second floor. When I am at my desk I get a good view of the city, which is great. The landlady, Signora Bianchi, is friendly and helps me with some of my language difficulties e.g. in the Petrarcan sonnets which I am studying at the moment.

As I make my way home to the Bianchis' from the university, here's my route: up the Corso Bersaglieri, under the gigantic Etruscan triumphal arch, past a group of Italian men playing a game of bocce, a turn to the right up Via Enrico Cialdini, past the grey-haired *lavandaia* (laundry women) scrubbing furiously at their washbasins, and, turning to the left on Via Guido Pompili, I see my apartment on the left. I haven't had any mail from you for at least a week so I curse the mailbox as I pass it in the hall. I climb the stairs singing softly *"Stormy Weather... since my gal and I ain't together/Keeps rainin' all the tiiiime."* I enter my room and...what ho! A letter from you! I have never got more pleasure from reading a letter.

Detail of "The Wise Men" by Piero Vannucci,
also called "Il Perugino". He was Raphael's master

September 5, 1960   Florence

Cara Fidanzata amata,

Here I am in Florence where I plan to spend about ten
days. I am writing this from an artist's flat with a terrace. I
arrived Saturday from Perugia after a hot and crowded train
ride. I had to stand for most of the 125 km. Hard lines! My
Greek friend Harry suggested that I look up a vague New
York girlfriend of his. I did, but she was out (in Greece,
to be exact.) A short mad-looking, bearded, sandaled, Van
Gough type from Trieste was bunking here, and as he had
no objection to my holing up for a while, I promptly did.
It costs nothing, so I can economize. Teo (the guy who's
staying here) is a talented sculptor: his busts of Verdi and
Beethoven are remarkably life-like and convey the power
of these two great men. He himself seems strangely uncon-
cerned about material things and literally lives from hand
to mouth, day by day. Quite often he goes without meals.

  The digs are good here: three large rooms. One
serves as a studio and is cluttered with paintings and good
books. The two American girls who live here seem to have
Medicean tastes. Their books cover a range of subjects:
history, art, travel, and literature. I always have in mind
that I should be studying Italian but I can't resist the urge
to dig into some of these excellent books in English. At
the moment I am reading (in translation) *The Etruscans*,
by Pallottino.

I really see now that to be in Florence is to be in the Mecca of artists. The city is about the size of Vancouver proper (400,000?) and is dominated in the center by the great cathedral dome of Brunelleschi's *Santa Maria del Fiore* and Giotto's bell tower. Much of the city is flat and the buildings which set the overall tone are light brown and in the Renaissance style. There are many churches of interest. When you walk around, the main impression you get is one of harmony and power. I would even add a feeling of denseness and confinement, not always, but quite often.

Santa Maria del Fiore (left), Giotto's bell tower (middle) and the Baptistry (right)

I spent Sunday browsing in the Galleria degli Uffizi, one of the largest in Europe. I was only sorry that you couldn't be there. Hundreds, yes, hundreds of originals by da Vinci, Michelangelo, Raphael, Titian, Giotto, Van Dyke, etc. Holy Smoke! My esthetic needs were gratified almost to the point of satiety! I also was impressed by the *Piazza della Signoria* where you can see *Perseus with the head of the Medusa*, *The Abduction of the Sabine Women*, *Hercules and Cacus*, and a very accurate model of Michelangelo's *David*. Truly a marvel!

In most of the churches and galleries here, especially the former, religious motifs dominate. In general the art is inspired by two very different (I would say almost incompatible) traditions, one Christian (Catholic) and the other pagan (mostly mythology). The art with pagan motifs charms me more than the Christian but the Christian art is more able to move me in a moral way. Menelaus, Hercules, Perseus. What great names! The religiously inspired works of Giotto, Leonardo, Michelangelo, and others make me want to find out more about Christianity and people like Saint Francis of Assisi and Saint Thomas Aquinas. Thank God for both traditions. Sooner or later I would like to study some of the technical aspects of painting: composition, design, and so on. I know so little about them.

Sunday evening I went to an open-air concert in an eighteenth century palace courtyard. One of the best trios in Europe, (Pelliccia, Santoliquido, etc.) performed. There they were, up on the stage and all around us were lush tropical plants and trees and Grecian columns and arches which cast eerie shadows. Add to the picture a colossal ornate fountain and further up, in the sky, the Tuscan moon, shining somewhere over Persia. When they played the first selection, Beethoven's opus 7, number 4, I came close to jumping up on my chair and shouting for joy!

On Monday I visited the Pitti Palace. This palace houses a famous jewel collection but the main attraction is the Medici art collection. The paintings are displayed in a crowded, helter-skelter way which is a bit overwhelming. I have never seen so many great paintings crowded into ten rooms. Paintings are organized differently in the Uffizi: they are not crowded and they are grouped together according to painter or genre. This gives a feeling of space and orderliness.

It also makes it easier to focus on one painting without being distracted. A nice surprise: I didn't have to pay for admission. My student I.D. card from the University in Perugia did the trick. A bonus.

Robert Browning's house, *Casa Guidi,* is right across the street from the Pitti and I had a good look around. This was his love nest with Elizabeth Barrett-Browning. The flat is furnished exactly as it was in the late 1800s. I found the atmosphere quite moving. I could imagine them reading sonnets to each other.

I almost forgot to mention the evening that I spent with Teo and two girls. We went to a big night-time festival on the banks of the Arno. There were thousands of people there, all of them carrying something that looked to me like a Chinese lantern. We arrived late but we heard the last of some singing. Everyone sang and it was quite strange and moving. On the river were hundreds of little boats with lanterns. The whole scene was lit up in blue, then grey, then white searchlights which were mounted on two of the bridges. There was a lot of energy, a *je ne sais quoi* in the air. You could sense the pride of the Florentines. I think the festival is called *La Rificolona*. **[5]**

The author standing under Perseus

Two nights ago, while wandering around the Piazza della Signoria, I was approached by an Italian who asked where Cellini's *Perseus* is. I took him to the other end of the piazza to see it and then translated into Italian for him some of the comments in my guidebook. It was a good exercise and gave me an idea: might it be possible to make a living here as a semi-professional guide? I forgot to mention: I just had a beer with a smuggler who is going to court for tearing down posters from public buildings.

Florence, Dante and Me

Everything in Italy is advertised by means of these posters (And they don't put up just one, they put up several, sometimes many.) This guy will probably get life!

I can't get over how good looking and well-dressed Italians are. I've yet to see an Italian female in slacks (or even a skirt, for that matter!). Invariably they wear dresses and almost always high heels. The hair styles are smashing! But what is most charming is the way they dress up their little darlings for public display: cute little two year olds in party dresses, with long hair and little earings. The little fellows are very masculine in their short pants, jacket and white shirt and tie. The men wear their hair slicked back in the pompadour style and, since it's still summer, wear white or light-colored suits. They almost always wear a white shirt and tie. At first their shoes seemed pimpish to me (pointed suedes, etc.) but now I'm used to them and think they're elegant. I intend to buy a pair as soon as the Italian government writes me my next cheque.

I had a political confrontation at lunch a few weeks ago. There were four of us: me, an Italian, an American and a Frenchman and we were all speaking Italian. The Italian said that Britain started World War II by interfering in Spain in 1936. This is rot on several counts. Britain never (openly) intervened in Spain although Germany and Italy certainly did. It was a convenient training ground for the Luftwaffe. I tried to make the point that Germany started the war by invading Poland when she had been warned that this would cause Britain to declare war. The whole thing was skewered and out of context. I then thought, "Oh, for the tongue of a Demosthenes! Oh, that I knew this language better, so that I could crush this churl! Don't they remember that without Britain and the Commonwealth (and the other allies) we'd be living now under the Japanese and Germans? Er, and the Italians, come to think of it. Anyway, to my utter incredulity, the American and the Frenchman agreed with the Italian. I thought that I must have stumbled on an Italian fascist, a French Pétainiste and an American isolationist! It was a bitter conversation and I hurried out of the restaurant with my stomach in knots and feeling like I'd like to beat their brains out. How can some people still fail to see the important issues in the last war?

The other day I could hear some Beethoven coming from the next apartment. I couldn't resist the urge to knock and say how much I was enjoying the music. It turns out that the guy who answered the door is from Montreal and had the same scholarship last year as I have now. His field is painting and he studied for a while under Arthur Lismer of the Group of Seven.

A book that I read at the American artists' pad was by Bernard Berenson, one of the world's greatest experts on judging from many little details if a painting is authentic. He has a lot of wisdom but sometimes he is out to lunch with his intellectualizing. Take this: "The Nazi uprising and aggression was due to a counter-Mediterranean revolt." Now isn't this the height of intellectual Bull? How about the militant ambition of Hitler and his Nazi party? Or revenge for the Treaty of Versailles? Berenson stayed in Florence thoughout the war at his villa (*I Tatti*) which I plan to visit. Yesterday at sunset I went up to the

Piazzale Michelangelo, the huge square on the south bank overlooking the city, and the view was an unforgetable panorama. Mussolini apparently took Hitler up there when the Führer visited Florence. *Und morgen die ganze Welt!*

I finally cashed my scholarship cheque yesterday, after walking from bank to bank for what seemed hours. You've no idea of what frustration is until you encounter this kind of bureaucracy. When I finally found a bank who would cash it they asked if I had a sponsor. "A what!?" I asked, steam coming out of my ears. "That's just great! No one in Florence knows me well!" So I went to see if the Canadian consul could help me. Guess what? There isn't one. Then I went to the British Consulate and explained my problem. A man from the Consulate returned to the bank with me and gave this *clericus magnus* a good dressing down. The chickens clucked a different tune when he arrived on the scene. I got paid off in huge five thousand lire notes (They measure about ten by six inches.)

September 16, 1960   Perugia

My dear J,

I arrived in a somber, grey-skied Perugia at 3 p.m. after leaving Florence about 12:30. I found summer's smiling face vanished and the sky threatening. It is indeed autumn and how well this dead season's gloomy days blend with the ancient dark stones of the city. How well this season suits my sadness at not having you here with me.

I wrote to you ten days ago about my trip to the Uffizi Gallery in Florence. I went again. Ah, the Titians! I spent about an hour there looking at his lovely *Venere Giacente* (Venus reclining) and must confess that I've fallen in love with her. Almost, that is. As the song puts it: "Strictly between us/You're cuter than Venus/And what's more, you've got arms!" (So don't be jealous!) There is so much great art to see in this gallery that I have restricted myself to studying a maximum of twenty works each time I go.

Thanks so much for sending the photos of you in Banff. I am the envy of all the Italians I show them to. *Che bella ragazza!* they say. *Ma guarda quelle montagne, proprio come le nostre Alpi!* (What a beautiful girl! But look at those mountains, just like our Alps!) *Fortunato Roberto!*

The other night I went to dinner with a few Americans and three Italians. A curly-haired, muscular Italian guy joined us after supper and played Neapolitan songs on his harmonica. We all got a little high and started to sing. I got so plastered I recited a French poem. We all had a pleasant time. Later we went to the apartment of one of the guys and continued to sing, a mixture of Italian and American songs. This went on into the early morning. After we left we Italian boys started playing soccer with a tin can in the street. We were really raising hell when sploosh!—some dame threw a bucket of water at us from the third story. Lucky for me, she missed! Her vehement expression of disapproval was, I thought at the time, highly Italian. I promptly showed my disapproval by rocketing the tin can at her window! Then wham! Smash! *Caspita!* (What the hell?!) Two bottles were hurled out of her window at me, narrowly missing me and smashing to smithereens on the pavement. *Attenzione!* (Look out!) I'm getting out! Incidentally, this happened not two blocks from where Browning's Fra Lippo Lippi climbed out of his cell window to partake in the festivities. I was very impressed with Andrea del Sarto's painting. Grays and blues predominate, as Browning justly observes, only I don't think his statement about Andrea's lack of inspiration is valid ("This forthright craftsman's hand of mine"). The faces on his madonnas move me.

September 22, 1960   Perugia

My dear J,

Two Italian friends just called on me: Giorgio and Odorisi. The latter, who knows Italian literature very well, asked for the names of some of my Canadian "girlfriends" with whom he could correspond. I gave him M's and R's addresses so please tell M and R to expect some letters in French. I helped them compose the letter and it was a good exercise for me to listen to their Italian and put it into French. Doing this takes me right out of thinking in English and somehow speeds up my learning. They are good fellows. This matchmaking might work out.

It seems strange to go to a movie here, e. g. *Fango sulle stelle* (Mud on the Stars) and hear Montgomery Clift speaking perfect Italian! American movies, especially westerns, and Perry Mason are very popular over here.

The bar where I go at least twice a day is an attractive place and puts me in a good mood as soon as I enter it. It's spotlessly clean, everything glitters, and there is such an impressive wall-full of exotic bottles to admire: from *Strega* (Witch), a liqueur, to whiskey. The fizzed up and sweetened warm milk is really good (and I never thought I'd drink the stuff!) And such pastries and cakes! My favorite is the *veneziana*, which is filled with whipped cream. Really, we have no imagination at all compared with these Italians when it comes to delicacies of this sort. And you should see the *baristas* in action. They are well groomed and prepare the coffee so swiftly—Tac!—and serve you with such flair.

Je souffre, je t'aime, je t'entends,

As I write this to you I can hear below on the Via dei Priori scooters and motorcycles roaring up and down. God, are they noisy! Italians and vehicles are an interesting co-phenomenon. Once mounted on a vehicle the Italian loses his earthbound identity and becomes an accessory of the vehicle, a speed and noise-crazed fiend! I guess futurism is a true expression of this. Of course I can analyze this until I'm blue in the face. I still find the noise damned irritating.

The other evening I went on an excursion with Jan Elderkin (from Vancouver) and several others to Città di Castello (Maybe forty miles north-east of here and up in the Apennines). It was part of the Umbrian Music Festival and the tour was organized by the University for Foreigners. The Prague Symphony Orchestra performed Mozart's *Missa Brevis* and Beethoven's *Ninth* in a fine old Dominican church. I love the simplicity of this architecture. In the *Ode to Joy* the resonant harmonies produced by the hundred strong chorus echoed throughout the ancient church. I was overcome, exalted and ecstatic! How can I explain this? I blessed every voice in the choir for an angel's. I'd travel to Milan to hear the Ninth done so well! After the concert we drove back to Perugia and went for drinks at the studio of one of the Italians. He had produced some interesting bark compositions (bark mounted on a painting and producing various patterns). He was a gigantic, bearded fellow and toasted the future success of his art. To me he seemed to have a typically Italian kind of personal pride and dignity. (I think the average Italian would sooner starve for a month than go without that smart new suit with the tapered, cuffless pants.) Coming home on the bus I sat in the back seat next to a Finnish woman and an Italian who were necking passionately. Ah, *triste amour* (or maybe I should say, *"Que je suis triste sans toi."*) There was a crescent moon shining over the silver Tiber. How I missed you!

Quand reverrai-je, hélas, de mon petit village
Fumer la cheminée, et en quelle saison
Reverrai-je le clos de ma pauvre maison,
Qui m'est une province, et beaucoup davantage?

When shall I see again, alas, of my little village,
The chimney smoke? And in which season
Will I see again that little plot of land
That is a province to me, and much more than that?

Joachim du Bellay, *Les Regrets*, sonnet XXXI, 1558.

Florence, Dante and Me

October 4, 1960   Perugia

My dear J,

Last night I heard a stirring open air band concert given by the Bersaglieri in the Corso Vannucci. They played *Capriccio Italien, Dance of the Hours*, etc. On the way home I bought a pizza to munch on. Two slices for guess how much? Sixty lire (ten cents).

The most memorable thing I've done this past week is to laugh my head off at Alfredo, a frigidaire salesman from Padua who stays here at the Bianchi *pensione*. He's short and stocky, built like a wrestler, with great sparkling eyes which reflect whichever mood or whim happens to pass through his quick mind. It seems we take at least two hours for every meal, what with singing and telling jokes (I do most of the listening.). Alfredo grew up in Sicily during World War II and remembers one thing very clearly: the Germans set up defensive positions on hill towns facing south, the direction from which the Allied troops were coming. They calibrated their guns to hit certain precise points, then blasted our soldiers to smithereens when they arrived at these points. After wreaking this havoc the Germans would retreat very speedily from the north end of town and set up a new position on the southern edge of the next town. It was all very clever and deadly. **[6]**

Alfredo has just bought a Fiat 500 so I am getting to see more of the city. We went to go for a drive the other day and he found that someone had spit a really nasty one on his windshield. This was upsetting for him and made me wonder who could have done such a senseless, spiteful thing. Alfredo's opinion of Mussolini is quite positive. In his words (which I have translated), "In Italy he did much good for the people and had many fine public works built. With his devotion and boundless energy he made us proud and united us for the common good. His biggest mistakes were to wage war in Africa and ally himself with the Germans." Maybe in time *Il Duce* will be looked on as a tragic, overly-maligned figure. Who knows? I have the impression that many Italians still cherish his memory.

The weather the past few days has been sunny, finally! September was stormy and wet.

Lorenzo, Signora Bianchi's son, is a tall, raw-boned, somber, silent, tough-looking customer. He is a keen hunter. From the outset he hadn't spoken a word to me and I got the impression that he didn't like me much. Then the other day, out of the blue, he gave me a copy of Dante's *Divina Commedia* which he said he had used in school. I don't believe he really used it because there is not one note or any underlining in the book. My guess is that he spent most of his time in the *Giovani Fascisti*, building a strong body and learning to think like a real fascist. If so, I guess that's not his fault. Anyway, I was touched by his gift. He has his heart in the right place. A second copy of Dante (with the clear commentary by Tommaseo) will come in handy. At Rachel Giese's suggestion I have been using the version with Momigliano's commentary. I am sick of it. It is certainly refined but it is also abstruse and unnecessarily complicated. Worst of all, he disdains to explain the concrete details of who, what, when and why. Tommaseo is clear and helpful and shows no such disdain. Lorenzo has done me a big favor, probably without knowing it.

The other night there were a few visitors here: a nine year old boy and his sister, five years old. Both are darlings. The boy got on my back and the girl climbed onto Lorenzo's back. A game of knock him out of the saddle! The next day I heard the little boy say to his mother, *"Mi hai visto sulla groppa del Canada?"* (Did you see me on Canada's back?) I was tickled when I heard this. I am getting used to being called *"Il Canada"*.

I have been getting together with a group of young Italians. We meet in a sewing shop (of all places!). We sing, dance and clown around in a small room about twelve feet square. They enjoy my Nat King Cole imitations. I hear that without exception women up to about age twenty-three are forbidden to go out unescorted after eight p.m. It would appear that there are some slightly frustrated young ladies— and young men, over here! I am told (by I forget whom) that this protects a girl's honor. Sounds like seventeenth century Spain to me but *Paese che vai usanze che trovi.* (i. e. No matter where you go you find different customs.)

Italians are so unpredictable. I was visiting Jan in the hospital the other day. A nurse came along and offered Jan a bun. When Jan said "No, thanks!" the nurse said *"Boh!"* (Meaning more or less: "Beats me!") then skipped out of the room merrily, tossing the bun up and down. Italian policemen take great pride in their job. They have the charming chivalric custom of tipping their hat after they talk to anyone.

I'm surprised to hear of George X using the term "Dogans". This is the Orangemen's term of scorn for Roman Catholics and I dislike it intensely. I hate nothing worse than the tendency of certain people to disparage all Catholics, as if they were all cut from the same cloth and as if Catholicism didn't have some very good aspects to it.

I was studying Dante the other day and as I was reading I heard the rollicking sound of an organ grinder from the street below. I jumped to the window, leaned out and there, strolling up the cobblestone street, was a little bereted Italian playing this merry song:

> Marina, Marina, Marina, ti voglio più presto sposar!
> (I want to marry you sooner!)

Is this song popular in Canada? The landlady here, Signora Bianchi, is a good sort. She laughs a lot, shaking her head from side to side. She helped me figure out a few of Petrarca's sonnets the other day. Her daughter is nice too and sings a lot. I came in for lunch yesterday and entering the dining room sang to them in Verdian style:

> È pronto il pranzo, signore? Ho una fame da lupo!
> *Is lunch ready, ladies? I am as hungry as a wolf!*

To which the daughter sang a reply:

> Sì! Prego, Signor Roberto, si metta a sedere!
> *Yes! Please, Mr. Robert, be seated!*

I had a conversation the other day with a German girl who said to me, "Verdi's and Puccini's music is inferior to Bach's and Schubert's." I argued that the genres couldn't be compared. Who has equaled Puccini's melodies such as *Un Bel Dì Vedremo* or Verdi's *Caro Nome*? Verdi is also a first rate dramatist (especially in *Il Trovatore* and *Rigoletto*). So he worked with melodramas! What's wrong with melodramas? What else can be made into an opera? Len Timbers in Vancouver once said to me derisively that opera is a "bastard art". [7] But why condemn it on this score? I ask. Of necessity it contains various arts: music, theater, poetry, and (often) ballet. If we condemn it for this reason we have to condemn ballet as well. I don't find his criticism meaningful. Let me sob for Puccini's tragic (and perhaps foolish) characters rather than smugly raise an eyebrow in disapproval. Of course I like the German and Austrian composers as well.

I had a chat with a South African girl who spent last year in Florence on the same scholarship as mine. I gather that these scholarships are world-wide. I think they are a great idea (I would, wouldn't I?). Before going to Florence she already had a B.A. in French and Italian. She said that the courses at the University of Florence are very difficult. She is the only foreigner who passed the exams last year.

I went to see *Les Béatitudes* at the Morlacchi Palace the other night. Although the presentation was good (Conductor, Marcel Couraud) what I found most impressive was the Morlacchi Theatre itself. It's like a small La Scala. It has dazzling gilt everywhere. There are six tiers of booths (each about the width of a sofa), intricate flowery designs on the walls, and immense white Corinthian columns framing the stage. Then you notice that someone has planted a little flower garden at the edge of the stage, a charming touch of nature. I felt that I was living in Mozart's era and got an inkling of what it might have been like to own my own elegant little theater. I am off to Rome in a couple of days and will keep you posted.

October 6, 1960   Rome

Cara fidanzata mia,

Here I am in Rome. I arrived about eight last night by train.
The trip down the Tiber valley was picturesque. I was struck
by the many hill towns. Suddenly you see one, proudly dom-
inating the hill on which it stands. I could hardly believe it
when we hit the northern outskirts of Rome for it seemed
like a surrealistic nightmare: thousands of new apartment
buildings that were lit up and cast eerie shadows; some
seemed to slope at crazy angles. This goes on for miles and
miles. Finally we arrived at the train station in Rome. It is
colossal and grand and, I'm sure, a monument to the glory
of Fascism and the Power of the State.

I will be here for at least a week and I am staying in
a *pensione* on the fifth floor overlooking a busy avenue (Via
Nazionale) and not far from the Colosseum. I am sharing a
room with a Siciliano named Luigi. He's an excitable guy and
probably very tough. We had lunch in the living room and he
took a roll from the plate, made a sour face and declaimed,
Questo pane non è buono! And whoosh! The roll went like a
rocket out the open window. I couldn't see where it landed
but someone must have got a surprise. (Maybe they thought it
was a miracle, maybe a re-enactment of the Israelites' manna
from heaven.) I could see nothing wrong with the rolls, by
the way. Luigi is from Trapani on the west coast of Sicily and
has invited me down there for Christmas. I'll have to think
about this. Certainly the *isola del fuoco* (the island of fire, to
use Dante's phrase) is high on my list of places to visit.

Florence, Dante and Me

Last night there was a full moon so I took a stroll down towards the Colosseum which is only a few blocks away. I've never seen anything with so much romantic-historical appeal. The whole area is lit up from the inside with yellow-orange lamps and this creates a chiaroscuro effect. Very poetic. Then there's Constantine's arch and the statues to Julius and Augustus Caesar. All are impressive. Trajan's column is most unusual. It's maybe fifty feet high and made of marble. Winding around it from bottom to top (in chronological order) is a bass-relief showing by many progressive scenes how the Romans carried out their conquest of Dacia (modern Romania). You can't make out much above the ten foot level and you would have to be a hummingbird with many hours to spare to inspect the whole column. The details of the bass-relief are amazing. How tenacious the Romans must have been when they laid siege to a place! And what a remarkable idea, to construct a detailed story of the conquest even when they knew that no one would ever see more than a fraction of it. I guess that didn't matter. What probably mattered to them is that they conquered and then celebrated the conquest in long-lasting marble. Who cares who saw it? And it would surely please Mars. [8]

It rained in torrents this morning and fortunately I had my smart new Italian umbrella. I had just passed the colossal church of Santa Maria Maggiore and was making my way towards the British Library when all of a sudden the downpour stopped and the sun blazed forth, causing myriads of rainbows and reflecting yellow-green light off the tropical plants. What a glorious sight! I will study Dante for a while then visit more places this afternoon.

*Trajan's column (top) and detail of Roman
soldiers holding heads of Dacians (bottom)*

A few days ago I went with Luigi to the Villa Borghese, which is set in a huge park with many tall, stately evergreens. I think they might be the famous pines of Rome that inspired Respighi's music. We planned to do a bit of riding and finally found the horses. Since we weren't "dressed", dontcha know, we were given the old 'ta-ta!' or "Get lost!" For the ostler's benefit Luigi put on a dumb foreigner's act. This was amusing because he's so Siciliano. We wandered around the famous (or infamous, depending on your political views) Via Veneto, where all the big timers sit at outdoor tables looking cool. The best time to go (to see famous actors, directors, celebrities, etc.) is apparently about ten p.m. I saw the famous Fontana di Trevi, the one we saw together in *Three Coins in a Fountain*. It is very grand and comes as a complete surprise because there you are, walking along a narrow street and suddenly, out of nowhere, you see it there before you. The streets of Rome are full of such surprises: you follow a narrow street and suddenly, completely unexpected, you see something very grand, like the Trevi or the Pantheon.

I visited the railway museum in Rome's train station. Four hundred twenty-five trains arrive daily. Just think of it! On display was an old (early 1800's) steam locomotive, with carriages, preserved like new. I felt like a Georgian squire as I mounted to sit in the plush red velvet seats of a first class carriage.

This afternoon is lovely and warm and the only thing that could bother you is the noisy scooters from time to time. Sitting here reading at my table I look up and into the eyes of a grinning lion (on the wall of a baroque building across from me). I think he's growling, "Get back to Woor-rrkkk!" So ciao for now.

[Later] It's midnight and I am sitting up in bed writing. Occasionally the Sicilian in the next bed either pounds his pillow, mimes something, or mutters some obscenity. We're good company. I went for a walk earlier this evening along the Tiber. There was a full moon over Castel Sant'Angelo, which in turn was ingeniously lit up from within, casting a golden veil on the billowy clouds. Then I walked over to Via Veneto. God, what wealth! Rows of people, mostly Italians and Americans I think.

The other day I visited the Vatican. Saint Peter's is immense, even bigger than I had imagined. I think I saw the Pope but it was from several hundred yards away and I can't be sure. Then to the Capitoline Hill to see the statue of Marcus Aurelius and Michelangelo's staircase. I had a good chat with the doorman at the museum. He was an Italian artillery officer and had been at Tobruk and El Alemein. I don't judge these people for fighting against us in the war; they too were victims of circumstance. I think they sense this about me and are very willing to talk about the war. Of course none of this would be possible if I didn't initiate the conversation in Italian. I'll sign off now. As I do so I hear a sky full of Roman crickets and, incongruously, a drunk singing at the top of his lungs in the whore-lined street below my *pensione*. I bet you could hear these same sounds in the days of the Roman Empire.

I went back to the Villa Borghese this afternoon but had only enough time for a once-over. I was particularly impressed with the Parmigianino, of which I sent you a copy. Like the Palazzo Pitti gallery in Florence, the Villa Borghese is crammed with Roman and Greek statues and Renaissance paintings in no apparent order. On the ceiling are frescoes of biblical scenes. I was touched by a statue to Lord Byron with a quotation (with which I agree heartily) chiselled in the stone:

> *Italy, the garden of the world and the heart of all that art can offer.*

Thence to the zoo, where I walked for miles and saw all kinds of strange animals. I fed a giraffe by hand, and as I did so felt the end of his tongue swoop down onto the back of my hand. Its tongue must be a foot and a half long. Weird. *Strano!* At the entrance they had two lion cubs and you could get your photo taken with them. I was very tempted but it cost too much. They were darlings. Other things of interest: eagles, cobras, pythons, crocodiles, strange baboons, camels—about every animal you can name, some four thousand varieties.

What I am going to say might sound really weird but here goes! Before I came to Italy (or Britain too) I think at some obscure, unidentifiable level I was not entirely one hundred per cent convinced that the ancient world actually had existed. In my mind it seemed a bit academic, unreal, and unconvincing. Oh, I had read about it and it *seemed* real but not *absolutely* real beyond any doubts or misgivings. I would never have admitted this to anyone because it sounds a bit loopy but I think it represents the truth of how I saw things. Maybe it has something to do with having spent my whole life up to now in a pretty remote, relatively recently settled corner of North America. What I am trying to get at here is that in Italy I have experienced things at a gut level, with real physical contact: I have walked in the Colosseum and touched its walls, I have pushed the great door of the Pantheon open with little more than a tap, I have walked the Via Sacra along which Julius Caesar rode in triumph to celebrate his conquest of Gaul. I see myself a little like "Doubting Thomas" who could only be convinced of Christ's wounds by touching them with his fingers. At the moment I harbor no doubts whatever about the reality of these ancient civilizations. I have changed and it has come about through real physical contact. My experiences in Italy are confirming everything I ever read about her ancient past.

Dr. Leonard Grant, professor of Latin, UBC

I am so glad that we took those two years of Latin with Professor Grant. As I wander around Rome I think from time to time of the things he spoke of: how the slingers from the Balearics carved insults in the lead projectiles that they slung at their enemy; how graffiti by illiterates gives us an important clue as to how Latin was probably pronounced; his detailed description of the swords, spears, armor, etc. used by Roman soldiers; how Caesar in Spain almost had a mutiny on his hands when he ran out of pasta for his troops.

Florence, Dante and Me

Dr. Grant is easily the best teacher I have been lucky enough to study with, ever. For me he represents the high degree of learning and the clear kind of presentation that I want to achieve. Maybe it's significant that he taught Latin in high schools before teaching at UBC. I especially appreciate the way he spent five minutes or so at the beginning of each class reviewing the previous day's lesson. It kept everything fresh in my mind. **[9]**

Here in Rome what has impressed me the most is the Pantheon, a colossal Pagan temple. It's located in a congested part of the city, with narrow streets and few, if any, wide vistas. So you are walking along one of these narrow streets and all of a sudden, Wham! you see the Pantheon. What surprises you is that it appears intact, as opposed to most buildings from ancient Rome which are more or less in ruins. To enter it you push an enormous steel door (twenty feet high? twelve inches thick?) but you don't have to push hard. Just a few fingers will do. This is *really* impressive. What kind of architects were these ancient Romans that they could make this possible? Then you go inside and you look up at the round aperture and through it pours a river of daylight which illuminates the many statues, pagan and Christian, which are located around the inside perimeter. How wise of the Romans to choose a name that no god (except the Jewish and Christian one) could take offense at. Now there's the practical mind at work: the safe approach. More than anything I've seen (with the possible exception of the Colosseum) the Pantheon gives you a feeling of what Rome was like at its peak: its beauty, its grandeur, its mystery.

The Pantheon

Rome's modern history is also interesting. Natch! I had seen photographs and film footage of Mussolini standing on the balcony of the Palazzo Venezia and orating to hundreds of thousands of Italians on the square below him. The other day I stood in that gigantic square, looked up at the balcony and imagined what it must have been like to be there in June 1940 when he pledged to fight alongside Germany. I could almost hear him. It gave me a strange feeling.

Yesterday I spent several hours reading CBC [Canadian Broadcasting Corporation] news reports at the Canadian Consulate. I wonder if one can subscribe to them. They are quite informative. The vice-consul was a French-Canadian, a very nice guy and easy to talk to. It is strange how my thinking about Canada seems to have changed now that I am in Italy. From here Canada seems somehow more unified, whole, and not a series of regions

Florence, Dante and Me

spread out from coast to coast who don't really know each other well. Also, and I don't know why this is, I think I am now far prouder of my country than I used to be. I am convinced that a deep love of our native land is not just a tradition which we are brainwashed with but a vital, worthwhile emotion which is like blood for our heart. The next time I hear "Oh, Canada!" played I will sing it with love and pride. I miss Canada at times: big things like having my own car and little things like the White Spot Triple O hamburgers and being able to take a good long hot shower whenever you like. **[10]** But there's a vitality in Italian life that is missing in Canada. You sense it walking down the street, in the proud way that people walk, the care and style with which they dress, the way they tend to express openly their emotions. Then there's the colors of the market, the book stalls—even little things like walking along a back street and hearing through an open window some music lover practicing the piano or violin. I shall miss these things when I am back in Canada. I am leaving for Florence in the morning. I plan to find suitable digs and enroll at the university.

October 19, 1960

Florence,
Via dei Serragli

My dearest J,

I have found what seems like a good place to live. It is
certainly cheap and it's got a pretty central location: a few
blocks south of the bridge, *Ponte alla Carraia.* This is not
a fashionable area to live in but I couldn't care less about
that. It has character and no signs of tourists or people
who sell to tourists. It's a working class area called San
Frediano. **[11]**

My local bookseller

Florence, Dante and Me

The church of Il Carmine (with Masaccio's powerful murals) is found in it. My room is small, maybe fifteen by ten feet. It has a single bed, a desk and chair, a huge *armadio* (armoire), a sink, a toilet, and a large *bombola* (gas cylinder) which heats up the room quickly. That's it! Pretty Spartan, eh? I am on the second floor and look out onto a *vicolo* (a very narrow street). Right across this street is a *vinaio* or wine-drinking establishment. Down the street only a block away there's a second hand bookseller who sets up his two huge book carts every morning. It looks like a good place to browse.

There are five of us staying here. First, Ede Parenti, the landlady. She's about sixty, a widow and a Florentine. Then there's Colonel (retired) Franco Cugiani, also about sixty and a Florentine. The third occupant is Gino A., a Neapolitan. He's about my age and plays violin in Florence's main orchestra. Then there's Magda, a *commessa* (salesgirl) in a clothing shop. She is from Arezzo and in her mid-twenties. Last: myself. The layout of Ede's place is a mystery to me. There are three floors. Magda's room is on the ground floor; Ede, Gino and I all have rooms on the first floor up; the colonel's room is on the second floor. None of us renters have cooking facilities so we eat out. Ede has a large kitchen and living room to herself.

There's an inner courtyard to the apartment so when you stand on the landing you can sometimes see your neighbors across the courtyard and to the sides. On the landing the other night I felt like singing so I leaned out over the courtyard and let fly with *Your Eyes are the Eyes of a Woman in Love* from *Guys and Dolls*. Magda was on her landing but when I started to sing she bolted into her room and slammed the door. I pretended that I was amused. I had an audience of eight or nine others who clapped and seemed to enjoy my performance. By the way, I have still not located a singing maestro but I will be working on it.

Gino   *Colonel Franco Cugiani*   *Ede Parenti*

Last Sunday afternoon I watched the landlady, Ede, and two of her friends play cards. This was fun. It's these insignificant little games and customs that delight me as much as *les grands spectacles*. I'm off to La Pergola Opera House tonight with a ticket to see Massenet's *Manon Lescaut*. I read the libretto today but find it trashy. L'Abbé Prévost would turn over in his grave, I think. Let's hope the music is better than the libretto.

I am hooked on Dante more than ever. He was a man of great passion and insight and he creates many strange, colorful characters. Just a few verses and you get the whole character and the drama of their life. In one scene Dante is walking with Virgil in the circle of the suicides and reaches out and unthinkingly snaps the branch off a tree. The tree cries out to him, *Perché mi schianti?* (Why are you breaking me?") It is Pier della Vigna, who was *consigliere* to the Emperor Federico II. Pier relates how he was unjustly accused and imprisoned, had his eyes gouged out and in despair dashed his own brains out on the stone floor of his cell. It took an amazing imagination to come up with this scene and hundreds of others like it.

In the fifth canto of the *Inferno* (the circle of the libidinous) Dante encounters Francesca da Rimini. She and her brother-in-law Paolo are doomed to fly around together forever, buffeted by a whirlwind. This is the punishment for the libidinous who do not believe in God. Here are the last lines that Francesca says to Dante after he calls out to her to speak with him:

> Ma se a conoscer la prima radice
> *But if to know the real beginning*
>
> del nostro amor tu hai cotanto affetto
> *Of our love you have such a desire*
>
> dirò come colui che piange e dice.
> *I will speak like one who weeps while speaking.*
>
> Noi leggiavamo un giorno per diletto
> *We read one day for pleasure*
>
> di Lancialotto, come amor lo strinse.
> *of Lancelot and how love seized hold of him*
>
> Soli eravamo e senza alcun sospetto.
> *We were alone and suspected nothing.*

Per più fiate gli occhi ci sospinse
More than once that reading caused us to exchange glances

quella lettura, e scolorocci il viso; (...)
and drained our faces of color;(...)

Questi, che mai da me non fia diviso,
This one, who will never be separated from me,

la bocca mi baciò tutto tremante.
my mouth he kissed all a-trembling.

Galeotto fu il libro e chi lo scrisse:
Galahad was the book and the one who wrote it:

Quel giorno in più non vi leggemmo avante.
That day onward we didn't read further.

They didn't read any further because Francesca's husband took them by surprise and killed them both. Dante sees in Francesca a kindred spirit: passionate and sensual, refined, well-spoken and well versed in courtly literature. At the end of the encounter Dante is so overcome by pity for them that he faints. *Caddi come corpo morto cade.* (I fell like a dead body falls.) One day I hope I can teach you to read Dante in the original.

Last Saturday I went to a supper party at the villa of two American artists (painters). They are good types, modest and hard-working. No airs about them. Leonard, (the painter from Montreal who studied with Lismer) was there. He annoyed the heck out of me by saying that Canadians are dull, materialistic people without illusions. **[12]**

A snooty South African woman agreed with him. I didn't get involved even though I was very irritated. The South African had some interesting things to say about her country. She thinks that a revolution of the blacks is only a matter of time. When there are scares from time to time she says that some whites practice machine gunning in their back yard.

Italy in October is rain, rain and more rain, very intense, violent rain. Twelve people died over the week-end because of the rain.

October 25, 1960   Florence

Donna mia ben amata,

I went to see *La Bohème* at the Pergola Theater last night.
Seventy cents to sit in the students' balcony! There were
lots of students there and they behaved like ill-mannered
children, I am sorry to say, and actually hissed during several beautifully sung arias. I was put off. The performance
was good. Mimi was pretty and had an excellent voice. The
falling snow in Act III actually looked like the real thing!

   I spent this afternoon at the Uffizi where I never got
out of the Botticelli room. When nature mixed the best of
artistic talents in one man, surely it was Botticelli! How to
describe his work? Imagination, tenderness, richness and
harmony, a perfect interplay of light and shadow? All these
he has to perfection. The huge Botticelli room is usually
packed with noisy guides and tourists but I was lucky enough
to find it empty for an hour. I sat in a chair in the middle
of the room from which I could see all four walls: *Pallas
and the Centaur, Madonna with Saints, Allegory of Spring,*
and, above all, *La Nascita di Venere,* (The Birth of Venus).
I could stare at this Venus all day. When I see something as
beautiful as this I am really moved. This is hard to explain
any other way and I know it might sound a little weird but
I get goose bumps, and sometimes a lump in my throat. As
I gazed at the face of Venus, so tender and wistful, another
beautiful work of art ran through my mind: Keats's *Ode on*

a Grecian Urn: "Thou still unravish'd bride of quietness,/ Thou foster-child of silence and slow time." I almost could hear Pan somewhere playing mysterious music on his flute. How powerful it is when one work of art triggers off memories of a work of art in another medium! What a strange age Botticelli lived in! To think that he complied with the puritanical Savonarola and, obsessed with a sense of sin, destroyed some of his own best work.

Two Botticelli's. Pallas and the Centaur (left) and the Birth of Venus (right)

I have started visiting the outdoor book stall just down the street. The owner is friendly and doesn't mind how many free reads I take. He has a completely unpredictable selection of magazines and books, which makes it fun. I was elated to find several opera libretti that date from about 1900. Their owners' names are on the inside cover. Mystery! I wonder who they were. These libretti go for only fifty lire (eight cents) each. The libretto Italian is often very antiquated and hard to follow, especially the one to *Il Trovatore.* **[13]**

World War II. Italian partisans fighting in San Frediano

The other day I bought a much better bike. Thank God! The old one was a real clunker. This one is a real racing bike and painted a lovely robin's egg blue. It just flies! Three gears! And only 12,500 Lire ($20.) I bought it from Ede's niece's husband, Signor Sgherzi, a friendly guy who makes fine furniture in his big workshop on the Lungarno a mile or so down the river from me. He specializes in *genuine* eighteenth century French furniture.

When I went to pick the bike up at his shop I noticed some scary photos on the wall. These showed a group of Italians, (men, women and children) with hands up and frightened faces being herded by very tough-looking, armed German soldiers towards a ditch where they will all be shot. This happened near here out in the countryside somewhere. You get a horrible feeling of helplessness and terror looking at photos like this but it's the reality of what happened in 1943 when Italy capitulated and the Germans took over. These photos were framed and they were up on that wall to honor the dead. No hiding the horrors of the war for these people! They lost friends and family. Maybe the most terrifying thing about those days is that people often couldn't tell whether they were talking with an anti-fascist partisan or a Fascist. I have heard that to avenge themselves for one German soldier killed the Germans would kill twenty or more people, often chosen at random. Twenty Italians would be rousted out of their homes then herded off somewhere, shot and left to rot in large hole in the ground. The brilliant Florentine, Machiavelli, would have seen the logic to it: if you can't rule by love, use terror. I have found an excellent magazine with authentic photos of the civil war in Florence (1943-44) and will show it to you when I come home. It's hard to imagine that these horrible things happened just sixteen years ago. I looked carefully at Signor Sgherzi's photos but didn't comment or pry because I thought it might be something personal that he definitely would not want to talk about with a stranger.

This spring I hope to take many trips with this bike into the Tuscan countryside. So many little hamlets and green valleys to explore!

[A note from 2017: The photo below is similar to the one I saw in Signor Sgherzi's workshop. The sign says *Sono questi i liberatori d'Italia oppure sono i banditi?* (Are these the liberators of Italy or are they bandits?) Some of these young men were probably partisans, some deserters from the Italian armed forces.] **[14]**

Italians being led out of town to be shot

I have seen two powerful movies on Italy in World War II and they are both 'musts'. The first is *Roma, Città Aperta* which gives a good idea of how the Nazis operated, especially how their agents weasled information out of naive Italians by pretending to be their friends, or simply had them tortured. The title is ironic: the city is not open in any sense; it is entirely under the Germans' brutal control. The second movie is *Paisà*, a series of six stories (or better, vignettes), of the allied army as it makes its way up the peninsula: the south coast of Sicily, Naples, Rome, Florence, a monastery somewhere in the mountains, and finally the marshy area of the lower Po River. The segment that takes place in Florence really fascinated me because it was shot right here during the war. This is one of the things that makes the Italian "neo-realist" movies so powerful— much of the footage was filmed under the very nose of the German army. Anyway, see them if you can! The director of both is Roberto Rossellini who was once married to Ingrid Bergman.

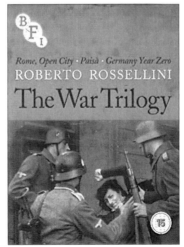

I enjoyed your last letter. Strange that you should suggest we try thought exchanges from a distance. I thought of this same idea just the other day. Let's experiment with this as soon as I find out the exact time difference. I think it might be eight hours.

Thanks so much for typing up extracts from these letters and showing them to a few of our friends, including several university professors (Yikes!). I simply have not had much time to write anyone other than you. In times to come these letters will serve as a reminder of my year in Italy and, who knows? maybe they will become the source of a book. I wonder if there are other students who have chronicled their year's stay in another country.

Right now I can hear Gino practicing scales on his violin at breakneck speed. Very impressive. The training at the Naples Conservatory must be very intense.

November 1, 1960   Florence

Dear J.

Hey, what gives? I haven't heard from you in two weeks. I feel like we're losing touch. I hope there's a letter soon! You comment on my lack of nostalgia for Canada. I guess you're right. I think I've convinced myself that you won't be joining me and that thinking nostalgically isn't going to make me any happier here. Quite the contrary.

Today is Armistice Day in Italy and also a day of campaigning for those people seeking election in the provincial government. For the first time ever party leaders are campaigning on television. I spent the afternoon prowling around *I Tatti*, the estate of the painting expert, Bernard Berenson. His villa in the north end of the town has been converted into a student residence. Maybe I can move there in the spring so that I can read Torquato Tasso on a marble bench under a palm tree. The gardens are lush, with many marble statues to admire. The estate is on a hill and below you stretches a panorama of Florence. It's magnificent.

Riding home from *I Tatti* on my beautiful new bike I ran into a big political rally. Can you imagine the Palazzo Vecchio in the moonlight, splendid in its crenellated rooftops, with rows of torches lighting up its turrets and below, surrounding the square, the shadowy figures of *Perseus with the head of the Medusa, David,* and *Hercules and Cacus*? And all of this with *fortissimo* march music in the background?

It was eerie, powerful and very medieval. I couldn't help thinking of Savonarola, this being the very place where that well-meaning Puritan was burned at the stake. Everyone I've met criticizes the Christian Democrat government but apparently none of the others are trustworthy either. It seems strange to see the sickle and hammer on banners. I've heard that the Communist party here is five million strong.

Well, the U.S. elections are on but I haven't had much time to compare platforms. My sympathies have switched from Kennedy to Nixon, possibly as the lesser of two evils. Certainly Kennedy's statement to Congress, "I would be prepared to fight an atomic war over Berlin." reflects rashness. With our Pearson I would avoid a nuclear war at all costs. Nixon has also traveled to dozens of countries in the past year and this impresses me. **[15]**

I've seen a few good movies: *Under Ten Flags* with Charles Laughton and *La Violetera,* a romantic Spanish story with a haunting theme song.

There are certain songs from North America that sneak into my mind from time to time. Strange how it happens. *Canadian Sunset* is one. It gets me thinking of the Rockies and you and that wonderful hike we took into Jasper's Tonquin Valley last summer. Other songs which sometimes pop into my mind are *Love letters straight from your heart* and *Mamselle* ("A small café, Mamselle/A rendezvous, Mamselle..."). A good song is a lyric poem.

An eager and completely crazy Italian friend of mine wrote your friend M a letter in French and I confess that I helped him compose it. What a lark! It will be interesting to see where this leads.

Florence, Dante and Me

I must record this now. I can't wait! Two tarantella dancers just went down the street, one dressed all in white, with a black mask, the other dressed as a drum major in red and black. They were accompanied by a bass drum and two accordeons. How frantically they danced! What a sense of fun and gaiety these Italians have! I leaned out of my window to watch them and saw my neighbors across the street watching too. I shouted and threw some coins into the street, which seemed much in keeping with their little festival.

I am getting in solid with "the family" here. The landlady, Ede Parenti, is a cheerful, roly-poly woman of about sixty and a few of her friends, e. g. "Tosca" come over here a lot. I spent today (Sunday) at Tosca's apartment. About eight of us were there, including Gino and Ede. It is in the center of Florence and (what charmed me) they have a rooftop garden with a sizeable fountain, many large potted plants and a cat who lords it over the place. The view is spectacular: Giotto's *campanile* (bell tower) and Brunelleschi's great *Duomo* are only a few blocks away. We listened to Luciano Taioli and Gigli records, drank vermouth, danced and had a good time. It certainly makes a difference in life when you get a few friends.

Ede has offered me the use of her late husband's study/library. His name was Dante Parenti, which seems fitting because I am studying so much Dante. It's a snug little room and you wouldn't even know it's there because it's hidden by a staircase. On the shelves I saw Carducci, Leopardi, Manzoni—all the classics—plus some very esoteric stuff. Her husband was apparently an inventor of sorts, one of his inventions being an astrological wheel contraption for tracing the significance of various constellations in our life. The room contains beautifully carved oak furniture which Dante made himself. He must have been a multi-talented man. This place has a spooky feel to it and at times I have the feeling that there is someone else in the room with me. *Molto strano!* What an honor to be allowed to use this sanctuary! Signora Parenti tells me that her late husband was a keen Dante scholar. I think I have just been admitted into a select club.

My courses at the university will probably be Dante, Foscolo and early Romanticism, history of the Italian language, translation (French, Italian) and nineteenth century French literature. The courses start on November 10. The Christmas holidays are long and run from December 22 to January 17. The academic year ends on May 30. Final exams are in June.

You quote someone who describes Boccaccio as "fresh, healthy and natural". I'm not so sure. There's a lot of violence, treachery, cheating, etc. in his book. I just finished one of his stories about a young Perugino horse merchant who travels to Naples and gets cleverly swindled by a whore.

I have to laugh at your stories of our friend R [spending the year in Paris] and her three showers a day. I go to the public baths one block away in Via dei Serragli every Saturday. These are curious places. You pay one hundred lira for admission and take a seat. When it's your turn a stout, stone-faced woman in a black outfit with a white apron (and a very no-nonsense manner) gives you

Florence, Dante and Me

a towel and soap and escorts you to your shower booth where you spend the allotted ten minutes in complete ecstasy. I have always liked showers but when you can afford only one a week they are pure joy. The rest of the week I splash around at the sink in my room. There is no hot water but cold water splashed on my face really jolts me awake in the morning.

A few weeks ago I got chatting in Italian with a friendly guy at the public baths. He asked me a bunch of questions about Canada. He's in his late twenties and married with two kids. I gathered that they are living in wretched poverty and feeling desperate. He asked if I could help him get into Canada. I told him that I would help him if I could but I didn't see how exactly. A few days later I heard some pebbles bouncing against my window (on the second floor). I looked down and there he was. He asked again if I could help. I had to tell him that I couldn't do anything. I felt awful. His distress is so deep. God knows how he makes ends meet. How lucky we are in Canada!

I am still working away at the spoken Italian. If anyone perversely insists on not understanding me I mutter some obscenities in English or I say to him *"Pazienza!"*

Enclosed is a photo of me taken on the Lungarno, the street that follows the edge of the Arno River on both sides of it. The Uffizi Gallery is only a block away. That's the south bank of the Arno in the background, and you can see the riverside railing. The massive pillars are part of the Uffizi complex.

In Italy men wear their trousers without cuffs. I am getting used to this style and like it.

The author

A few evenings ago I saw a film, *Il Dittatore Folle* (The Insane Dictator). I was appalled by the scenes of Jewish persecution. The footage of the mass Nazi rally celebrating Hitler's fiftieth birthday were eye-boggling. Mussolini must have thought he couldn't lose in becoming an ally of such a powerful nation.

November 6, 1960   Florence

Dearest J,

I took the train down the Arno to Pisa yesterday, a ninety minute trip. Pisa is flat and much smaller than Florence. The Arno flowing through it lends it charm. The leaning tower is a bit scary to walk up and when I was about half way up I decided to come back down. I saw the houses where Byron and Shelley lived but they were closed to visitors. Pisa is the first place where I have seen major World War II bomb wreckage to buildings. Seeing actual ruins sure brings home the terrible, useless destruction caused by that war. Apparently they are still finding unexploded bombs in the countryside. I have seen several warning signs of them. I went into a bar in which people were watching a soccer game on TV. Someone scored and you should have heard the hooting and waving of arms. These Italians!

Italy taxes some things that we don't. If you have a private telephone you are allowed only two free calls a day. After that you have to pay six cents per call. Radios are taxed $20. a year.

Italians seem to find themselves in a galling situation: they receive low wages and have to cope with a high cost of living. LP records, for instance, cost double here what they cost in Canada.

Pisa

If you don't come and join me in Europe next summer I will be very disappointed. I would probably return to Vancouver and work (if there are any jobs) or take a course or two at UBC summer school. Yet there's so much I want to see and do in Europe if I had another year here and you here with me: read Dickens in a downtown London garret, spend a summer reading and going to Shakespeare's plays at Stratford-on-Avon, spend a few months in Dublin reading Joyce, visit relatives in Scotland and see Macbeth's castle, live in Paris for a few months and take in the impressionist galleries—all this plus whatever else your fertile imagination cares to suggest. Your letters do more for my morale than anything else. Mother often spends a whole letter discussing such fascinating, world-shaking topics as to whom will she give the apples in her back yard! I know, I should be more tolerant.

Florence, Dante and Me

Milan after the bombardments;
Pisa and Florence were badly hit as well

You say you find the idea of eternity "a tiring prop-osition". I can't really imagine eternity either but I don't conclude from this that there is no eternal life or, if there is, that it would be boring. If Mozart, Verdi, Dante and Shakespeare are up there and willing to socialize it's going to be very entertaining. I hope we don't die forever. I can't think of anything more useless or depressing than the idea of dying completely. There has been so little justice on earth throughout the centuries. Are evil people to get away with their wicked deeds? Will there be no reward for virtue and sacrifice? Are the great martyrdoms to be rewarded only by the stake? I can't believe it, or *feel* it, and on this subject I think that feeling is the only basis on which to decide. In short, faith, not reason, nor philosophy. I really dislike (and even resent) your likening Christianity to a crutch. This implies that to be a Christian is to be a weakling. That is false. It takes enormous strength to be a real Christian. At the same time, I have to admit that I have not known many real Christians in my life.

I came across something in T.S. Eliot the other day which I think puts our argument in perspective:

> Man is man because he can recognize supernatural realities, not because he can invent them. Either everything in man can be traced as a development from below, or something must come from above. There is no avoiding that dilemma: you must be either a naturalist or a supernaturalist." (From *Second Thoughts about Humanism*).

I don't propose for a minute that this proves man's immortality but I prefer to believe in an afterlife as opposed to nothing. It's too bad that our positions on religion are so different. Putting aside the question of an afterlife I still think there is much to be gained by finding out what Christianity has to say about values. Looking back on my schools and family I realize that there was almost no discussion of the Bible or values. Realizing this

Florence, Dante and Me

has come as a jolt and I have Dante to thank for it. His system of Hell is constructed largely on the basis of the Seven Deadly Sins (pride, avarice, gluttony, lust, envy, anger, and sloth). Before I discovered Dante I hadn't even heard of them. I now realize how much damage pride (the arrogant kind), for instance, has caused in my own life. How arrogant and full of myself I have been at times! I cringe! I can remember in grade twelve my stepfather was bed-ridden with very painful shingles for a whole month. I don't think I visited him once. How horrible of me! I was so self-absorbed! And I know there were people in high school who thought (rightly) that I was full of myself. One of the horrible things about pride/arrogance is that when people see it in us they hate us on sight. Anyhow I look forward to probing deeper and deeper into all of this. I feel that I am on the right track. In Italy reminders of the Bible and its moral values are all around you: in the cathedrals, the countless small churches, the art galleries, and above all, in Dante's poem.

Another question we have touched on is when to visit Europe. Like you, I have always favored the idea of reading extensively before going to Europe but now I don't think it matters much if we 'miss' things on the first visit for lack of formal training in history, painting, etc. I get overwhelming esthetic pleasure (and I am learning all the time) from going to almost any gallery or church in Europe. This satisfies me for now. I can always return again and again in the future and, through study, appreciate more and more each time. I look forward to studying the history of art and the technical aspects of painting when I have the time.

I find something else is happening: my taste in painting is becoming more and more confident. Now I can go into a gallery room with fifty paintings and with a quick glance around the room zero in on the few that I find really good, and interesting. I think I am usually right in my choices. I certainly didn't have this confidence or ability when I first came to Europe. The first gallery I saw was the National Gallery in London last August. I can remember being very impressed with Leonardo da Vinci's *Virgin of the Rocks*. If I looked at it now I am sure I wouldn't be anywhere near as impressed. I have seen many paintings which I think are much better. Without realizing it I guess I have been learning what to look for and what to discard.

Two portraits by Il Bronzino

This new faculty that I am acquiring seems to be carrying over into other areas: buildings, statues, land-scape, even clothes. Can experience improve one's taste?

Florence, Dante and Me

I definitely think so. Oh, I have picked up useful information from books but most of what I have learnt about art has been through experience and learning to use my own judgment.

I have discovered *Il Bronzino* recently and for portraits I think he's the greatest. I don't need to take a course to find out how great he is.

By the way, you mention that you are studying *The Charterhouse of Parma* in Woodcock's course on the European novel. **[16]** Why not study *I Promessi Sposi* (The Betrothed) by Manzoni? He is considered the Italian Walter Scott, more or less, for his ability to portray people in the Lago di Como region in the seventeenth century. Much of what we study (and are taught to revere) at college depends on the personal choice of a professor or department committee. I'd sooner base my choice of what to read on what a whole nation cherishes and feels close to the heart. Such a writer is Manzoni for the Italians and maybe Charles Dickens for us. I also prefer to develop my own taste without prompting by academics who have developed their own (often conventional?) tastes. Remember first year French and having to plough through Molière's *Le Malade Imaginaire*? I think it was a stupid choice (all that silly bathroom humor about blood-letting and enemas!) when you consider how it pales beside *Le Bourgeois Gentilhomme*. What brilliance! There's the kind of play we should have studied.

Another great discovery for me in Florence is Michelangelo's bust of Brutus in the Bargello (now a museum, formerly a jail!). Such intelligence and strength of character in this bust! I have never seen a more noble face. I find it strange that Dante puts Brutus in the bottom part of Hell where he is stuck forever in one of Lucifer's mouths and chewed away for all eternity. He's classified as a traitor to his benefactors. It's not easy to understand some of Dante's judgments. I see Brutus as a noble defender of the Roman republic.

Michelangel's Brutus
(in the Bargello, Florence)

Florence, Dante and Me

Dearest J,

Here I am at the *Università di Firenze* (not the University for Foreigners; this one's meant for Italians and would-be Italians like myself). It's five p.m. and I am sitting in an empty classroom. The professor will get a big surprise when he pokes his nose in the door and sees only my grinning mug. Only three people showed up for the course on Medieval philosophy. The lecture was so complicated that I understood maybe twelve sentences. He recommended a number of books, one in English, which pleased me: Copleston's *Thomas Aquinas.* Sooner or later I am going to have to read Saint Thomas and Aristotle. Both were apparently major influences in Dante's thinking.

I have been thinking about what I have achieved so far in this year in Italy and what I hope to achieve from here on in. I think I can divide this into four parts:

MY PLAN FOR THE REST OF THE YEAR

1   Travel around Italy. I have traveled quite a lot: a week in Rome, six weeks in Perugia, a day trip to Pisa. Also trips to Urbino, Pesaro and Città di Castello. I want to continue traveling around Italy as much as possible without going bankrupt.

2   Take courses at the university. I have taken a month or so of courses at the *Università per Stranier*i in Perugia

and I am now starting courses at the University of Florence. I am hoping to pass these courses in June and, I hope, get credit for them towards my honors degree in Romance languages from UBC.

3 Study Italian literature on my own. I am pretty pleased with my progress. There are big rewards to this study: through Dante I am learning to appreciate the medieval world. More important: studying his *Divina Commedia* has led me to explore my own conscience, especially my own sins and shortcomings, which I have usually ignored. These are pride (and the things that go with it: arrogance, self-centeredness, and insensitivity), anger (especially harboring grudges and thinking about vengeance) and lust. It feels right to be thinking along these lines. Surely the most important thing in life is to become a better person and to achieve this we have to judge ourselves honestly and become aware of where we fall short. I realize now that I grew up in a family that was more or less amoral. My brother and I never once went to church with our parents; the Bible and moral issues were almost never discussed. The public schools I attended also seemed to avoid moral issues. I grew up without acquiring the habit of looking at myself (and other people) from a moral perspective. I now think that I was in my own *selva oscura*, Dante's dark wood of the spiritually and morally lost. **[17]**

4 Study art, geography, history and politics. I have visited many churches, museums, galleries, etc. and will continue to do this.

5 Spend hours and hours talking with my intelligent, open-minded landlady, Ede, and the others with me

here: Colonel Cugiani (a great fan of Dante, Dickens, etc.) and Gino, my Neapolitan friend in the next room. Magda keeps to herself.

Guess what! Vittorio Gassman has become a close friend. I have bought a small record player and a 45 rpm of Gassman reading highlights from the *Inferno*. I listen to Gassman over and over and over, following the lines in my text and repeating out loud with him. I closely imitate every syllable and try to copy the rhythm, the music of the phrases. Without even trying I am starting to memorize large chunks. In the zone reserved for traitors Dante meets up with Ugolino, who betrayed and was betrayed in turn.

La bocca sollevò dal fiero pasto
He raised his mouth from the fierce meal,

quel peccator, forbendolo ai capelli
that sinner, tearing away at the hair

del capo ch'egli avea di retro guasto.
of the head that he had destroyed the back of.

Poi cominciò: "Tu vuoi ch'io rinovelli,
Then he began: "You want me to tell again

disperato dolor que il cor mi preme,
the desperate grief which weighs on my heart

già pur pensando, pria che io ne favelli.
just thinking about it, before telling the tale.

Thus begins the famous episode in Canto 33 of the *Inferno* where Dante encounters Count Ugolino (a treacherous character who is getting even with the Archbishop Ruggieri who betrayed him and had him and his sons locked in a tower and left to starve to death) who is gnawing away on the archbishop's cranium. Dante's lines, like Shakespeare's (which I had no difficulty memorizing in high school—reams of them!) somehow seem easy to memorize. I don't know exactly why this is, because they are both difficult, complex poets. Maybe it has to do with the fact that the words are so well chosen and none are superfluous. Maybe it's because both poets have a unique style—you have to hear only a few lines to know who wrote them. The musicality of the lines and Dante's complex, tight-knit *terza rima* also help. **[18]**

Gassman reads from Dante's Inferno.
Cover of the 45 rpm, 1958

Vittorio Gassman. What style!

I enjoy noticing the impression I make on people, since our Canadian way of thinking, dressing and expressing ourselves is different from the Italian way. Over here I think I appear a bit unusual, maybe even exotic, what with my *pizzo* (Van Dyke beard) and tartan vest.

In Canada I was more reserved; here I feel free to be more outgoing . Maybe that's because I realize it's up to me to be myself and reach out to people. I have to do it and I do. I had lunch with a guy at the university the other day and we got talking about poetry. He was an eager student of English poetry and I just happened to have some Keats on me so I read him a few poems with feeling. He was delighted and said to me: "You play with the words! I have not heard poetry read that way before." This guy never had the money to even think about an academic career but quit school early in order to apprentice himself in a trade. My impression is that he is gifted and should be at the university. There is something wrong with the system, I think.

I am now dreaming in Italian, which was a long time coming. A good sign. The first time I did this (about a week ago) was an exciting event. I woke up and thought about my dream and started analyzing it out loud in Italian. As I was doing this it suddenly occurred to me, *O Dio, ho sognato tutte quelle cose in italiano!* (Oh, God, I dreamt all those things in Italian!). What a strange process is thinking and words! What really amazes me is how words and phrases (often in French and Italian) pop into my mind out of nowhere. They come to me swiftly and without any effort on my part. I think they must come from the subconscious mind or maybe intuition. Whatever the source I find they are always right on the mark. Music pops into my mind in a similar way.

I forgot to tell you about Italian trees. They are so different from our trees in the Pacific Northwest. In Rome I was surprised to see so many palm trees. Here in Tuscany there don't seem to be any. The tree that dominates the landscape is the cypress: tall, slim and dark green. You see them often in paintings by Tuscans like Leonardo da Vinci. I wish I had more time to learn about plants and the stars.

November 17, 1960   Florence

Cara mia,

How pleasant it was to wake up to a knock on my door this morning. It was Ede (who has the same droopy, hooded eyes of Puccini—maybe they're related) with a café latte for me and, more important, a letter from you! I am glad to hear that everything is going well and that you are enjoying the acting.

I didn't tell you this but I have an excellent schedule at the university. My earliest class begins at ten. This suits me fine because I seldom go to bed before one a.m.

The weather here has been rainy for several days now and it gives the city a cold, gloomy aspect which tones in well with its age. My two mile bike ride to class every morning is an adventure. I carry my bike downstairs then hop on for the ride, balancing a portfolio and, if it's raining, an umbrella. I'm off! It's up the street (*Via dei Serragli*) a hundred yards then onto a steep incline up to the bridge, *Ponte alla Carraia*, one of several beautifully arched bridges across the Arno. I cross the Arno, which is often enveloped in morning mist, and looking upstream I catch a glimpse of other famous bridges: *Ponte Santa Trinità* and the *Ponte Vecchio* with its many shops. Zooming down the other side of the bridge I pass a traffic cop, in uniform and white-gloved, who directs traffic with real panache and has courtly salutes for some of the ladies. I turn to the right and follow a narrow, cobbled road until I reach the *Piazza dell'Indipendenza.* I proceed northeast for a few blocks to the *Piazza del Duomo,* which I circle to the right, almost crashing into a car next to me because I have been admiring Brunelleschi's cathedral too intently. At the northeast corner of the roundabout I enter the wide, busy *Via Cavour* which I follow for about half a mile until it flows into a large square, *Piazza San Marco.* I have arrived. I park my bike here, lock it, and enter the corner bar for breakfast: a veneziana pastry and a cappuccino.

Florence and her bridges as seen from the east. My bridge is the far one

On the east side of *Piazza San Marco* is the entrance to the church of San Marco and its cloisters. It is an eerily quiet sanctuary amidst all that traffic. The university's arts faculty is on the south side of the piazza.

As we've discussed, I think your desire to read scads of stuff before coming to Europe is not the ideal approach. I prefer to plunge right in and experience everyday life while I explore the galleries, churches, residences of famous people, etc. And it is only since coming here that I appreciate how puritanical Canada is. I used to dread Sundays. I actually studied most of the day! Bah! Here in Italy we go to house parties or public dances. We eat extra pastries in the morning and socialize during the day. We throw books aside.

My vicolo. My room is at the top left of photo.
The door to the vinaio is behind the man on the right

My quarter is old and dusty, with little beretted men joking in front of the corner wine shop, a little boy in tweeds playing an accordeon on the bridge, and a grinning guy named Abdul (his parents are Tunisian) puffing on a Florentine stogey (a *lupo*) while standing self-contentedly in front of his green-grocer's stall. And there, kiddy-corner I see, not exactly a wolf, but a huge muzzled wolf-like dog, probably from somewhere up in the Apennines.

Last night was most enjoyable. I went with Ede, my landlady, to see *Madame Butterfly*. Rosetta Noli played Butterfly. She has a lovely voice and made the part look easy, which it isn't. The set was charming: real cherry trees, bright silk costumes, parasols, etc. Do yourself a favor and listen to *Un bel dì vedremo,* Butterfly's statement of faith that Pinkerton will soon return to her from America. Only Puccini could write such poignant, heartfelt music. You need hear just a few bars to know it's him.

It's five a.m. and I just awoke. I am suffering from insomnia a lot, especially last night when I got to thinking about not seeing you for two years if I stay here and you stay in Vancouver. Anyhow, I awoke this morning convinced that I was in Vancouver then went back to sleep and cursed myself (in my sleep) for having left Italy. I would like to hear Freud interpret that one! Ede just knocked at the door, brought me coffee, and quoted a few lines of beautiful poetry. She's amazing. She got a big kick out of the *Ti voglio bene!* that you wrote on the envelope of your last letter.

November 30, 1960   Florence

Hello, J Dear,

I just got back from an afternoon in Empoli, a small town
about twenty miles or so down the Arno on the way to Pisa.
It was a bright, spring-like day and I went with the Colonel and Ede to see a re-enactment (in medieval costumes,
with horses) of the war conference which was held after the
battle of Montaperti (1260, a few miles from Siena) in which
Farinata, the victor, convinces his Ghibellines to spare Florence and not raze her to the ground. Long golden trumpets,
swords, standards, halberts, bright colored costumes—it was
quite a show. They read out loud Canto Ten of Dante's *Inferno*
in which Dante (a White or moderate Guelph) encounters
Farinata in the circle of the heretics. Farinata is lying on his
back, agonizing in a fiery coffin but when he hears Dante
talking to Virgil in Italian (with a Florentine accent) he begs
him to stop and talk with him. Dante does. They soon realize that they belonged to opposite parties and start arguing
bitterly. Here are Farinata's first words to Dante (before he
discovers that he is a Guelph). They are not easy to translate
but I'm sure you will appreciate the nobility of the language,
the concision and power of the lines. Farinata refers to Florence as his *patria*. This shows how powerful the city state was
in the minds of people during the Middle Ages. I try to keep
this in mind when I visit cities in Italy. The pride in one's city
of birth is still there.

Program for the Farinata celebration in Empoli

O, Tosco, che per la città del fuoco
Oh, Tuscan who through the city of fire

vivo t'en vai così parlando onesto,
alive, go about your way, thus speaking modestly,

piacciati di restare in questo loco.
May it please you to stay in this place.

La tua loquela ti fa manifesto
Your speech reveals you to be

Florence, Dante and Me

di quella nobil patria natio
of that noble fatherland (Florence) a native

alla qual forse fui troppo molesto.
to which maybe I was too harsh

It was an exciting experience and I'm grateful to Ede and the Colonel for tipping me off and taking me with them. They are watching out for the Dante-loving Canadian.

The hardest word in English for some Italians to pronounce is "world". It's fun to watch them try. The strange faces they pull! Oranges from Sicily and Sardinia are now in season. I noticed some at the fruit-vendor's. These oranges are blood-red and just looking at them makes me want to visit those islands.

December 4, 1960   Florence

Dearest Muse,

Like the ancient Romans, Italians have a taste for horror.
They like melodrama and they love westerns. The wild
west is really big over here and Alfred Hitchcock and Perry
Mason are popular. There is some censorship, which bugs
me. I saw a movie the other night which really shook me up:
Luchino Visconti's powerful *Rocco e i suoi fratelli*. (Rocco
and his brothers). It's about a poor, fatherless family who
leave the deep south of Italy in mid-winter and move to
Milan. There are four brothers and they all have to use
their wits to survive and get ahead. Two of the boys become
good boxers and fall in love with the same woman. She
might be a hooker of sorts, but that's not clear. In any event
she's intelligent, beautiful, has great charm and bewitches
the two young men. They end up having a horrific fight
over her. This hit close to home for me because of my own
family background and my years as a human punching bag
for a much older brother. I won't tell you more about the
movie or I'll ruin it. This movie is a 'must' and has been
nominated for an academy award. It's realism at its best
and shows the tight-knit loyalty of a southern Italian family
and their struggle to survive in northern Italy. Alain Delon
gives a first class performance as Rocco.

I have now read about twelve of Boccaccio's tales. I
am changing my mind about him. To many he might seem

scandalous but I must admit that I enjoy seeing where and how the various characters get seduced, tricked, or beaten up. Try Book III, tales one and four for a sampling. There are lots of parallels between Boccaccio and Chaucer. They are almost contemporaries but Boccaccio seems easier to me. His style is much closer to modern Italian than Chaucer's English is to modern English.

Rocco in the middle with two of his brothers

The damned inconsiderate bums! As I was having supper at my usual trattoria last night three young North Americans entered, two women and a man. They drank three liters of wine and smoked 150 cigarettes (The waiter told me he counted them!) Anyway, these three got all boozed up and emotional and laughed and cried and during their four hour supper had only one thing to say to the waiter: *Niente da fare!* (Nothing doing!). They were pathetically proud of this aggressive little idiom and used it on him several times throughout the evening. Can you beat this for sheer insensitivity and stupidity? These are the types who give Americans and Canadians a bad name over here.

With the exception of the Canadian CBC, Italian radio stations put ours to shame. They offer everything from German lessons to *Rigoletto*. By the way, I hope you borrowed the LP of *Madame Butterfly* from the UBC library. I was stumped by the word *celia* in the libretto but, sure enough, the colonel was able to explain it to me. It means 'playful and jesting'. I'm sure you'll like this opera as much as you do *Porgy and Bess*. It's just as real and the music as good, if not better. Even if you don't understand the words, you'll understand the emotion: the joy in loving and the pain of waiting for your loved one to return. (We can sure identify with that, eh?) It's all expressed so beautifully and the words and music are a perfect fit. You can't beat Italian for this last aspect, can you? No wonder it's considered *the* language in the world for music.

I have splurged and bought a huge hard-cover Italian dictionary, the *Palazzi*. It's not bi-lingual, it's strictly Italian only. It's coming in very handy and I am consulting it all the time. The beauty of an 'Italian only' dictionary is that you learn not only about new words, you also learn from the Italian in which the definitions are formulated. In short, you are drawn holus-bolus into the realm of thinking completely in Italian. English gets lost in the process and doesn't interfere. Another feature I love about this dictionary is the pictures it uses to teach words in a thematic cluster, so to speak. You learn the names of the objects in a typical dining room (*piatto:* plate; *bicchiere:* glass; *zuppiera:*

Florence, Dante and Me

soup tureen; *posata:* cutlery; *mestolo:* ladle, etc. The photos are old-fashioned which gives them charm. The editors of the Palazzi are openly nationalistic and they are quick to point out the gallicisms, anglicisms, etc. which they say are to be avoided. It is refreshing to read a dictionary that dares to be subjective. It's a bit like our Dr. Johnson and his digs at the Scots, the Whig party, etc.

A typical illustration from the Palazzi dictionary

I agree with you: we are branching into different areas in the humanities what with your interest in English literature and theater. However, isn't this more of an advantage than a disadvantage? We will be able to consult each other for information. I will always love English literature.

I am trying to get into the habit of studying at the Marucelliana Library but it's noisy. The way many students read out loud drives me nuts. I am caught between a rock and a hard place because I find my little room at Ede's too confining to spend all that much time in.

Bacchus by Caravaggio

I am sending you a portrait of Bacchus by Caravaggio. Isn't he decadent? **[19]** I've seen these very same eyes on some of the people I have met in Italy (including, come to think of it, Ede). And can you resist the wine goblet, that purple Chianti? I find this painting completely pagan and can see nothing Christian in it. I have seen a great deal of art and (as I mentioned) I find that it's helpful to think in terms of pagan versus Christian. Purely pagan art glorifies the senses and appeals to them. It is proud of being sensual and self-indulgent. It leads us, as Hamlet says, "down the primrose path to dalliance." Christian art tends to deny the senses and sensuality. It advocates self-control, self-denial, virtue, prayer. It helps me a lot to understand a painting when I remember to place it in its pagan-Christian context.

I found this description of Chianti in a guide book by Nannetti and thought you might like it: "Chianti has a good ruby red color, a harmonious taste, and a slightly bitter flavor." That nails it down, don't you agree? But I should know—I drink it twice a day. You get some surprises in Florence. I went into a clothes shop the other day and the salesgirl was a dead ringer for one of Botticelli's beautiful, ethereal blondes: the delicate features, the wistful look, the long wavy blonde hair. Okay, I'll stop!!

I went to a dance the other night. How I wished you were there! The orchestra was very good. They played some rumbas and some Argentine tangos. *Molto romantico.* The singer (tenor) was good and sang many of the latest hits such as *Marina* and *Piccola.*

A few days ago I visited the National Museum here in Florence. They have an impressive display of armor, swords, daggers, etc. Best of all was a fresco by Giotto which included Dante and his much-loved teacher, Brunetto Latini. I spoke with one of the guards who told me that his ship was torpedoed in the shark-infested waters of the Indian Ocean in 1942.

Do you remember Rick Bronson from last year?—the athletic guy who rode his Italian racing bike everywhere and who was absolutely determined to be an Italian. He used to say "Pronto" when he answered the phone, and that was in Vancouver, for gosh sake! You might have seen him in the halls of the Buchanan building or maybe at Nina Rossa's Italian restaurant. Always on the go, always with his racing bike and backpack. Anyway, guess what? He's over here! Yup, I bumped into him the other day at the Marucelliana Library. [20]

Caravaggio was a thrilling discovery.
Here is his "Doubting Thomas".

December 9, 1960   Florence

My dear J,

I am learning lots at the university: lots of Italian and lots about literature although they do like obscure polemics about the meanings of words and they attach too much importance to odd-ball intrepretations of literature which don't even deserve consideration e. g., Voltaire who dismisses Dante with two words: a "mathematical poet". Imagine reducing all that marvelous poem to two little words. He does the same thing to Shakespeare, calling him *un barbare de génie.* I am still studying a lot at the elegant Marucelliana Library.

The library is okay except for the talking out loud at the tables and the peculiar habit many Italian students have of reading softly but audibly out loud (I don't know where they get this.) There is a lot of talking at the movies too (and smoking, en masse, if you would believe!) Italians take the idea of personal freedom too far at times. If you mentioned these things to an Italian he might say, *Me ne frego!* (I don't give a f...) *Fregare* is the f-word. Almost anyone seems to use this expression and it doesn't seem to be considered vulgar. I hear that Mussolini liked to use it, I guess to show what a macho man he was. The trouble is, if you use an expression containing this "damned if I care" attitude it probably causes you to embrace that attitude even more.

The Marucelliana Library

I am getting to know Colonel Cugiani. He is widely read in history and literature. I just discovered that he loves Dickens and that made for an immediate bond between us. He also knows Dante very well and holds him in great esteem. It occurs to me as I write this that one thing Dante and Dickens have in common is an amazingly creative imagination. Scrooge's dreams are like something out of *La Divina Commedia*.

The colonel leaves here every morning at eight, dressed in a suit, coat and fedora and carrying a brief-case. I assumed he was off to work somewhere but I was told that he goes to a local bar where he reads newspapers all day. Speaking of characters! Where else but in Italy? Underneath the conventional image of the well-dressed man he's an eccentric and eccentrics seem to flourish over here. I guess I could say that most of the people I have got to know in Italy are eccentrics. As I mentioned, Italians are very well dressed and maybe this has something to do with it: if you are well dressed you command a certain amount of respect and as a result can feel free to act eccentrically and be eccentric.

Gino and I have become close friends. He is going to Barcelona with the Florentine orchestra and I saw him off at the train station at two a.m. He has invited me to spend Christmas with him and his family at Torre Annunziata, located about fifteen miles or so south of Naples. I had plans to ski in Switzerland with your friend R. and a few others so I am not sure now which I'll do.

It's funny how customs are. When Gino bought me a beer I thanked him, at which he took offence. I think his thinking goes like this: "By thanking me you have acknowledged that you feel obligated, but there's nothing to feel obligated about because this is a kindness that I am doing for you as a friend, because I like you. Also, I get pleasure in doing it so there is no need to thank me. I guess the converse applies: when I pay for someone's drink I shouldn't expect to be thanked! *Paese che vai usanze che trovi.* (Whichever country you go to has its own distinct customs.)

I bet that Communism will destroy itself long before Capitalism. Look at Hungary.

I can get the *Guardian* [*Mancester Guardian*] here for thirteen cents. No need to send me any. I am teaching English two hours a week at The Linguists Club.

Italians help solve the unemployment problem by creating work. No waste bins in the street and many people throw stuff on the ground. How is it then that the streets are clean? There is a whole army of mustached men with brooms. Maybe this is not a bad system.

I try to avoid dwelling on the negative aspects of this year abroad but they do exist. I have seen much poverty and wretched housing and, in Florence at least, a lack of those free public amenities which would go a long way to making life more pleasant for everyone. I mean such things as public libraries where you can actually sign books out. Also, indoor swimming pools (I know of only one.). I came to Italy full of romantic ideas about what it's like to live here. These ideas were fostered by the music I had grown to love (from Caruso to Carlo Buti) and by the Hollywood movies I'd seen (*Roman Holiday,* etc.) The trouble is, the characters in these movies are not cash-strapped scholarship students like myself but rather wealthy Americans who live high on the hog. Even Gregory Peck's apartment in *Roman Holiday* is super deluxe compared with my little monk's cell on the south bank of the Arno.

By the way, I haven't heard if my scholarship can be renewed for a year but I hope it can because, as much as I miss you, I am learning (and growing in many ways) so much over here. I am learning a lot about the Italian language, customs and ways of thinking; I am also furthering my knowledge of the arts: literature, music, painting, sculpture, etc. It's very lonely at times but overall the experience is well worth it. At the same time, I see clearer now some of the attractive things that Canada has to offer: more job opportunities, higher wages, better organized universities, not to mention hot tubs to soak in, hot showers and White Spot hamburgers. [21]

Giotto's St. Francis preaching to the birds

I find that they're ruining poetry for me the way they teach it: obscure polemics and an endless dissection of words. No expressive oral readings. No discussion. The professors make absolutely no effort to ask students for their impressions. I'll really be peeved if they give Dante this treatment. They certainly did nothing inspiring for the charming, powerful little poems of Saint Francis of Assisi. How in tune this man was with natural things and how filled with gratitude he is! The English version can't hold a candle to the Italian:

Laudato sii, mio Signore, per frate Fuoco
Praise be to thee, my Lord, for brother Fire

per il quale ci allumini la notte
through whom you illuminate the night for us

ed è bello e giocondo e forte.
and he is beautiful and jocund and strong.

Last week I studied practically nothing for my courses but spent many hours on Dante's *Inferno* and Davidsohn's very detailed history of Florence (I am reading an Italian translation from the German. Colonel Cugiani brought it to my attention and lent me the book.) The part from 1260-1321 fits in well with a study of the *Inferno*. Overall, though, I can't seem to get interested in the complex in-fighting of the Medici family.

I stumbled upon a very good definition of allegory: organized symbolism.

December 16, 1960   Florence

Mia carissima J,

Today is a *festa,* the Feast of the Immaculate Conception
and I rode my bike twelve miles up into the Apennines to
visit Rick Bronson. The trip takes you in the direction of
Bologna (north-east) to a point just south of San Piero.
You pass to the north of Fiesole. Much of this country is
wild and wooded, part of a game reserve, and you climb
to an altitude of about twenty-five hundred feet. I could
see rows of mountains in the distance to the northwest,
some covered in snow. I passed the *Grotta della Madonna,*
a cave with a statue to the Madonna in front of it. Nearby
is a waterfall and an ancient broken down mill beside it.
God knows how old! It could be from Dante's time. I can
well imagine him trudging along this very road at the
beginning of his life-long exile from Florence. Maybe it
goes as far back as the Romans, or even the Etruscans!
You can feel the history over here. It's mysterious and
powerful. The trees are bare, except for the cypresses
which are everywhere. The steep hillsides are thoroughly
cultivated.

   The *contadini* (farmers/country people) are wide-
eyed and suspicious at first but friendly once you start
talking with them. They dress more colorfully than the
Umbrian *contadini* in their drab black outfits and they have
a dignity in their bearing which impresses me. It's amazing

to see how they have increased productivity by cutting terraces into the steep slopes. When I arrived at Rick's he showed me how many farm houses you can pick out when you look really closely. (They are of the same color as the soil and difficult to pick out because of this.)

From Rick's you can see both Fiesole and Florence way down in the valley. We visited a few of his neighbors and watched them milk cows. The clean country air and healthy stench of the animals made me want to burst out singing in praise of rural life, maybe *Campagnola Bella,* as sung by Carlo Buti. *O campagnola bella, Tu sei la reginella!* (Oh beautiful country girl, you are the little queen! Ach, translations!) This song is on the LP record that I bought last year at Len Timbers' store in Vancouver.

I love Buti. His interpretations inspired me to memorize several of the songs on that record. I think it would be great if I could stay with a family of *contadini* and work on the land for at least a few weeks before returning to Canada.

Rick's wife is tall, woodsy and red-headed. She has learned to cook like a real *Italiana.* We had steak. Ecstasy! Oh,

A recording that taught me a lot of Italian

so tender! I haven't had a steak for months because my budget won't allow it. We listened to the Kingston Trio *(Hoist up the John B's.sails!/See how the main sails set!/Call for the captain ashore! Let me go home!)* and that sure brought back fond memories of you and that unforgettable week last summer in Jasper. Just as I set out down the hill from Rick's to return home my brakes gave out (a good thing I wasn't going forty miles an hour down a long steep hill!). He very kindly gave me a ride back to Florence in his van. It was good to see someone from home.

December 23, 1960   Florence

Idol mio,

A lot has happened here in the last nine days.

Gino surprised me by telling me his family can't have me spend Christmas with them because his mother took sick. They say that they'd like to have me stay a week or so starting the sixth of January. That's good news but I really wanted to go somewhere special for Christmas so I've decided to go to the Swiss Alps (Grindelwald) on my own. I might stop at Milan on the way back. If I'm going to be alone at Christmas I might as well be in a beautiful, exotic place. I wish you could go with me!

After visiting Rick and his wife (December 16) I realized that I had a week to do as I pleased so I decided to do a whirlwind tour of several northern Italian cities: Bologna, Mantua, Verona, Padua, Venice, and maybe Ferrara and Ravenna. [See map at the beginning of this book.] This was a pretty sudden decision so I didn't get time to tell you about it.

I took the train from Florence (December 17) and was in Bologna in an hour or so. (It's about fifty miles north by north-east.) The train cuts right through the Apennines: beautiful mountains, quite unspoiled, with streams and ancient mills. There you are, admiring the mountains, then Wham! You are suddenly on the southern edge of the great flat plain created by the flooding of the Po River. You are in Bologna, the site of one of the oldest universities in Europe (older than Oxford or Cambridge), the birthplace of Marconi, and a stronghold of the Communist party.

Bologna is also famous for its food and traditionally Italians call it *Bologna la grassa* (Bologna the fat.) The pasta does seem good and for some unknown (to me) reason it is usually a light green color. I soon found a good trattoria; my magic phrase worked once again: *Scusi! Dove si mangia bene e si spende poco?* (Where do you eat well and spend little?)

I had heard that Bologna gets a lot of fog in December. I don't know how true that is but it's proved to be right on this visit: I arrived to find fog and rain and it's been raining for the past few days. The city's architecture doesn't have the elegance of Florence but I suspect it had hell knocked out of it in World War II. There are many monuments to dead partisans here, something I haven't seen in Umbria or Tuscany. Maybe it's just me but in Bologna the memories of the war seem to be still in the air. I find the people friendly and several have gone out of their way to point the way to a street or a museum for me. They don't seem to say *Arrivederci* much, but *Di nuovo.* There are lots of people in the streets but I have hardly seen one tourist here. I don't know why this is.

Bologna was once Etruscan and there is a lot of good Etruscan stuff at the Civic Museum which I visited yesterday. Many of their figurines have droll smiles on their faces and I get the impression that the Etruscans were a happy people. I saw some very large swords and lances. Some of the large swords were unbelievably light. I tried wielding one and flashing it around until a guard told me to desist.

An Etruscan couple on their tomb at the Civic Museum

I visited the house of Carducci, the famous and much-loved poet who lived here. His house has been preserved intact, completely furnished, from the last century. There are forty thousand books in his library! I also visited the National Gallery. It's rich in somber Counter-Reform painting. It also has Raphael's *Santa Cecilia,* which I like a lot. There are dozens of rooms in this gallery and each one has a guard. Many of these guards sit there reading a *libro giallo,* which is more or less like Mickey Spillane. [22] One of them told me that he earned 46,000 lire a month. I was shocked to hear this. I get a stipend of 60,000 lire a month.

I know I am usually pretty cautious about where I stay but I threw caution to the wind and slept for two nights in an abandoned tower. I had heard about it from Giovanna, a friend of Teo the Florentine sculptor.

Two towers: the Garisenda (48 meters)
and the Asinelli (97 meters)

A few students were there with their sleeping bags and they had rigged up an old stove. They made me feel welcome so I decided to stay. I spent a few hours drinking wine with them and answered questions about Canada. They were quite interested. It turned out to be the creepiest night I have ever spent. I was sure that there were ghosts. Doors would slam but there would be no one there. Windows rattled and at times I could hear footsteps in the corridor.

Being in Bologna I just had to see the tall Garisenda tower to which Dante likens the giant Anteo. This takes place in the deepest part of the *Inferno,* canto 31, line 136. He describes looking up at Anteo, (who is rushing towards him with evil intent) and says that it reminded him of standing under the leaning Garisenda Tower and looking up at it as clouds (coming from behind the tower and towards him) sweep over it. I tried this and it works. What an image for his poem! I really felt that the tower was going to fall on me.

Mme. de Stael wrote that traveling is the loneliest of occupations. How true this is! I'd add that the loneliness is generally proportionate to the benefit derived because only alone can you do exactly what you want to do.

Overall Bologna was well worth the visit but I would like to see it again when the sun is shining. That might make all the difference.

My next stop was Mantua. I foolishly tried to see all of it in one day. It can't be done, as I found out. The city has canals, which surprised me, and some very ancient-looking skiffs floating on them. I guess it's all part of the Po navigation system. I visited the magnificent Ducal Palace. The highlight is the *Camera degli Sposi* and Mantegna's frescoes of the Gonzaga family. The faces of the Gonzagas are a study in pride (the arrogant variety). One of the rooms in this palace was designed for the court dwarfs and has stairs which are only about three inches high. Very cute. This palace is supposed to be the setting for Verdi's *Rigoletto*. Dante's mentor Virgil was born in Mantua and I sat in a stone chair which is supposed to have been his. This was a thrill.

A canal in Mantua

When Dante is threatened by wild beasts (a leopard, a wolf, etc.) in the dark forest at the beginning of the poem, Virgil appears and Dante asks who he is. Here is Virgil's reply:

Non omo, omo già fui
(I am) not a man, I was a man once

e li parenti miei furon lombardi
And my parents were Lombards,

Mantovani per patria ambedue.
Mantuans in origin both of them.

Nacqui sub Iulio, ancor que fosse tardi,
I was born in the time of Julius (Caesar) although late in his life,

e vissi a Roma sotto il buon Augusto
and I lived in Rome under the good Augustus

nel tempo de li dei falsi e bugiardi.
In the time of false, mendacious gods.

I wandered around the open air market and spotted a guy pinching an orange, very expertly. I wondered what would have happened to him if he had been caught. As I wandered the streets I remembered that Romeo comes to Mantua, buys poison from an apothecary, then returns to Verona to visit Juliet's family vault, kill himself and be with her forever. When I read the play in grade twelve I wondered what Mantua looked like. Now I know!

The Mantovani speak a dialect loaded with gallicisms. I wonder if it's a legacy from Napoleonic times.

I took the train to Verona, which is about twenty miles north-east of Mantua and situated on the northern edge of the Po Valley. The Adige River flows through it and looking north you get a spectacular view of the Alps. Unfortunately the art gallery was closed so I set out to track down Juliet's house, the house of the Cappelleti or "Capulets". In the courtyard you can look up and see the famous balcony. On the wall there is a plaque with a lovely quotation:

Florence, Dante and Me

But soft! What light through yonder window breaks?
It is the East, and Juliet is the sun!
Arise, fair sun, and kill the envious moon
Who is already sick and pale with grief
That thou, her maid, art far more fair than she.

I found it very moving to see these words in my native English. Somehow the lines seemed so right and I had a strong feeling that Shakespeare might have been here (no matter what historians surmise).

The Roman amphitheater is huge and well preserved. I got chatting in Italian with a museum guard and noticed that he turned to a friend and said, *Sì, sì, hai raison.* What a strange mixture of Italian and French! It would be interesting to find out more about these dialects which seem to be all around you here, wherever you go. I visited Juliet's tomb in the Capulet vault. It was silent and mysterious: only a few birds twittering and the rustling of some Lombardy poplars. I was the only one in the tomb and just had to recite Paris's challenge to Romeo near the end of the play:

Stop thy unhallowed toil, vile Montague!
Can vengeance be pursued further than death?
Condemned villain, I do apprehend thee:
Obey, and go with me, for thou must die.

The verses I declaimed echoed resonantly throughout the vault. Like Romeo, I too had just come to Verona from Mantua (only I wasn't bringing any poison with me).

The following day I took the train to Vicenza, stopped for a few hours and heard a mass and sermon in the *duomo.* I was soon on to Padua. *Padova la dotta* (Padua the learned) as the Italian saying goes, I guess on account of its ancient university. In the Scrovegni Chapel I saw some excellent frescoes by Giotto. His people have a kind of spiritual strength—a nobility and simplicity to them. It's hard to explain, you have to see them. (See p.99.) His figures are a big step forward from earlier painters such as Cimabue. These frescoes, thirty-six of them, deal with the life of Christ. They are not as well preserved as the Assisi Giottos but they are still well worth seeing. I tried unsuccessfully to find the Teatro Olimpico so I went into a bar and listened to music for an hour or so. The barman had a phonograph and very kindly played records for me (*Night and Day* by Sinatra was the highlight.) I am moving on to Venice (*Venezia)* tomorrow. This for me is as exciting as going to Constantinople or to the moon for that matter.

I arrived in Venice about noon. From mainland Italy you take a train out onto a causeway which leads to the lagoon on which the city is built. Lucky me—after several days of rain the sun was shining brightly. This city seems to float! You don't hop on the nearest bus, but the nearest boat! I was impressed with the Doge's palace (lots of Tintorettos and Verroneses, both of whom I like). There is a large room full of medieval armor and a sizeable collection of huge medieval swords. I walked over the Bridge of Sighs and entered the horrible dark dungeons to have a look. I saw Saint Mark's Cathedral (grand and impressive) and walked for hours around the city, over many little bridges, down narrow side streets, stopping at a whim, and finding the scene before me constantly changing. [23]

I really resent the rotten English translations of many guide books. At least ten errors per page! Before publishing why didn't they have a native speaker of English correct the manuscript? The guides I meet usually assume I'm French (and sometimes German) and speak to me in French. I answer them in French, then quickly switch to Italian. I never let on that English is my native tongue. There wouldn't be much to gain by doing that. I am not here to give them practice speaking English!

Leaving Venice and heading south I stopped briefly in Ferrara. Only a few hours, just enough time to see the castle of the powerful Este family and walk around town. One of the paintings in the castle depicts cock fighting, a sport which (so a guide told me) Italy introduced to the English. That was news to me. Then I moved on to Ravenna, where Byron lived for a few years and where Dante is buried (much to the annoyance of the Florentines who would love to have his remains.) Given the way they treated him (exile for life) I don't think Florence deserves to have them. The Byzantine frescoes in the churches of San Vitale and Sant'Apollinare Nuovo (fifth and sixth centuries) are magnificent and like nothing I've seen in Italy. Light greens and yellows (real gold!) predominate. The faces are simple, spiritual and very stylized. These two churches impressed me overall as much as any I've seen in Italy, including Saint Peter's in Rome and Saint Mark's in Venice. I had no idea that this was all part of the Byzantine Empire (capital: Constantinople, also once known as Byzantium, now Istanbul). Overall, Ravenna seemed flat, dusty and deserted. I returned to Florence via Faenza, a three hour trip.

San Vitale, Ravenna

So there you have it. I am glad I took this tour. I saw much of north-east Italy and I now have a better idea of the amazing variety of beautiful and interesting places to see in this country.

January 1, 1961   Florence

Happy New Year, Love!

It's six p.m. on a dark rainy Sunday and I am still recovering from a big dance last night at the University Club. I didn't get in until five this morning. They had a good little orchestra and played some of my favorites (*Ebb Tide, Blue Moon, I only have eyes* for *you,* etc.). Italians love rumbas and they played several. My ballroom dance course with Mr. Vincent at UBC two years ago came in mighty handy. No one else seemed to know how to do the real international ballroom rumba although Italians are good at improvising to any kind of music.

This afternoon I went to a gathering at Tosca's apartment. We played cards, listened to music and ate some fluffy kind of Christmas cake. It went well with the liqueurs. Tosca's lovely big cat presided. I forget his name but judging by his markings it should be "Boots". On the way to Tosca's I noticed all kinds of shoes in the streets. I asked someone about this and he said that it's customary to throw a pair of used shoes out the window on New Year's Eve. It's supposed to bring good luck.

A lot has happened in the last week. First, my skiing trip to Switzerland. On December 23 I took the train to Interlaken then switched trains to head east, up to Grindelwald deep in the Swiss Alps. The mountains are spectacular, even more so than Banff or Jasper. I rented

some skis, put them on, and realized with some trepidation
how much like an albatross I felt on them. "Bah!" said I,
"I will take the Gondola to the top of a really advanced
run." I did this then skied from the top of the lift over to
the beginning of the run. Before charging down the run
I made a few steps forward to see what it looked like. I
gazed down, and down, and down. Down into the most
terrifying precipice I have ever seen. I understood what
David Balfour felt like in Stevenson's *Kidnapped* when he
discovers that the top of the tower is unfinished and that
his uncle meant for him to plunge to his death. Feeling like
a regular chump I literally side-stepped down the whole
piste, step by step, slowly. Humiliated but wiser. I skied a
lot on gentler slopes for the next few days and enjoyed it.

I stayed at the Kirchbuhl Hotel even though at nine
dollars a day it's a bit steep. Beer costs thirty cents a pint
and is it good! Most people spoke German but a few spoke
Italian and I made some good connections with them. A
common language really bonds people (even if my Italian
is acquired). For supper one evening I shared a table with
an Englishwoman who said that she couldn't stand Botticelli or Michelangelo but that Giotto had "good line". I
was boiling in my soup at her remarks and attitude but I
held my tongue. Why spoil a good supper? I thought. Later
that evening I sat in the lounge and ordered a beer. I had
a parcel with me that my parents had sent from Canada. I
had assumed that it was a Christmas present and wanted
to savor the opening of it. "I wonder what this can be," I
chortled to myself. "Doubtless a nice little surprise." It was
a surprise all right: my old military hair brushes and an old

shirt. I had forgotten that I had asked them to send these things to me. I had to laugh but a bit bitterly. So much for Christmas presents!

One evening there was dancing and a guy played the piano. I enjoyed his rendition of *Winter Wonderland* in German. If ever there was a winter wonderland it has to be Grindelwald, believe me. A few of the men wore *lederhosen* and performed some Bavarian dancing. The following day was bright and sunny and I rented skates and did some ice skating at a large open air rink.

One night I walked into town from my chalet. I have never seen the stars so clear and bright. You could see the lights from little cuckoo-clock, wood-carved chalets shining in the valley and looming close in the night all around were the great hulks of the Alps. I felt serene and humbled and sensed strongly a power much greater than myself.

I don't remember exactly how it happened but one evening I got into a big argument with one of the hotel staff (a sort of manager) and it escalated to the point that we were going to get physical. (I might have had too much beer.) Anyway, neither of us was going to back down. It turns out I didn't have to risk it because a few of my Italian friends barged in and physically restrained both of us. Apart from this one guy, who was very obnoxious, I found the people quite friendly. I made friends with a German couple who live in the Black Forest. They invited me to spend some time at their place. It was nice of them and The Black Forest had such a mysterious ring to it that I was sorry to have to decline. I was running short of money.

After leaving Grindelwald I stopped for two days in Milan. I visited the *Duomo* and was astounded by how massive and intricate it is. I walked up to the roof which is absolutely flat and quite extensive. From there you can see all over Milan. In the evening I took in Prokofiev's *Cinderella* at La Scala. I was so thrilled to be in the house of the great Verdi. The Brera Gallery had some beautiful things, e. g. Mantegna's poignant painting of Christ laid out after the crucifixion: *Cristo Morto.* It's very realistic—you can see clearly where the nails pierced his hands and feet. One sees some strange things in galleries: I saw a small painting of two brigands slaughtering a couple of monks in a forest. There was snow on the ground. The brigands are fully clothed and one of them is clearly aroused as he is stabbing the monk. Is he aroused by killing people? Sick, sick, sick! Sant'Ambrogio is the patron saint of Milan. I saw his skeleton (dressed in high ceremonial robes) in the crypt of the church that bears his name. Not too appetizing a sight, I can tell you. He had not trimmed his nails for a long time.

Leonardo's *The Last Supper* is a moving sight. It occupies a large wall in the church of Santa Maria delle Grazie. The colors are pretty faded but I have heard that they are going to restore it (this takes years, for some reason). Leonardo uses chiaroscuro well and the colors are rich, but somber and unusual. They are also quite faded. Photos on the church wall show how the church was practically leveled (by our bombs!) on August 16, 1942. Miraculously, *The Last Supper* survived intact. In the evening I saw a movie, *The Apartment*, with Jack Lemon. The dialogue is fast paced and I missed quite a bit but still enjoyed it. It satirizes corruption in the business world. Lemon is a good actor. It looks like this movie is going to be nominated for all kinds of awards. It's funny to hear Lemon speaking Italian.

In the morning I took the train back to Florence. Snow had fallen on the Apennines and they were covered in white. A beautiful sight. In the train I shared a compartment with an Italian family. The mother asked me if I was from Florence. I was very pleased to hear this question! I guess my spoken Italian must be humming right along. On the few occasions when I speak English I have to admit that I come out with some things that are not quite right and sound strange.

So here I am back in Florence. It's good to be back. The gang here at Ede's were all pleased to see me and I was greeted with enthusiasm and warm hugs. Today, as usual, I went to have lunch in my trattoria which is just down the street. It's run by a cheerful elderly lady who calls herself "Italia". She has a loud voice and sounds like a hoarse raven. She's a merry soul and loves buffoonery. When I entered her *trattoria* today she hailed me dramatically, for everyone to hear, in that strange voice of hers:

Ecco il Canadese! Credevo che fosse perduto in un ghiacciaio in Isvizzera!

Behold the Canadian! I thought he got lost in a glacier in Switzerland!

Her pasta is flavorful and *abbondante*. Usually I sit at the same table as another regular, Mario. He's an artisan, highly skilled in manufacturing elaborately scrolled silver cigarette lighters and cases. He told me he was nine years old in the summer of 1944 and remembers well when the first British and Canadian tanks arrived. The fighting was tough as the Allies struggled to penetrate the Gothic Line, the tough German defensive line which ran through Florence. Mario and I get into long conversations, which teaches me a lot about life here and, incidentally, the spoken language. He has a theory that the Etruscans were a fun-loving people. Mario's a good type: intelligent, cheerful, and curious about life. He says my accent is like Mario Lanza's. I guess that's a compliment but I am not sure just how great a compliment.

Italia at her trattoria.
I see her as Etruscan

Filippo and his mom,
Italia

I had a beautiful surprise last night. The Colonel knocked on my door, handed me a parcel and said that he'd found it on the dining room table and that he thought it might be for me. Then he walked off, a faint *Buon Natale!* (Merry Christmas!) echoing from the dining room. It was a beautiful hard cover book: *Il Paesaggio*

Florence, Dante and Me

italico nella Divina Commedia (The landscape of Italy in *The Divine Comedy*). It contains over two hundred tastefully selected photos, from Sicily to the Alps, of specific places mentioned by Dante in *La Divina Commedia*. With each photo is included the passage in Dante's book which refers to the place. The photos include many subjects: cities, villages, towers, burial monuments, mountains, battlefields, harbors, etc. These are not pretty postcards in color meant for tourists, but real photos, almost all of them in plain black and white. This is the real Italy in its stark beauty. What a pleasure it will be in years to come to be able to look at these photos, especially when I am reading Dante. I am pleased to have already seen several places illustrated in the book: the canals in Mantua (which I told you about), Verona, Venice, Padua, Urbino, Pisa, Perugia, Fiesole, Castel Sant'Angelo and the Vatican, etc. This book might even be rare; it has been out of print since 1921. **[24]**

There is a friendly dedication on the inside leaf:

Firenze, Natale, 1960

All'amico canadese Roberto, amico di Dante,
To the Canadian friend Robert, a friend of Dante,

L'amico fiorentino Franco Cugiani
The Florentine friend, Franco Cugiani

in segno di stima e di affetto.
as a token of esteem and affection.

Cover of the book   The Colonel's dedication

Isn't this the ultimate in generosity, friendship and good taste? I also got a little leather diary from Ede. It came with a sprig of mistletoe and a dedication: *Nessuna nube turbi la tua fronte serena!* (Let no cloud disturb your serene brow!) How nice! She has the soul of a Romantic poet.

Good news: it looks like I will be going to Gino's (just south of Naples), leaving here January 6th. I am really pleased that this worked out. I am so curious to see Naples and Torre Annunziata.

A gift arrived from my brother in Vancouver: an LP of highlights from *La Bohème and Madame Butterfly.* I have been playing them a lot and everyone here loves to listen to them.

January 4, 1961   Florence

My dear J,

Yesterday I rode my bike up to Torre del Gallo, situated
on a hill to the south of Florence. Leaving by the Senese
gate, I made my way up winding, hair-pin turns, stopping
often to drink in the fresh country air and admire the lovely
panorama of Florence, towered and domed, nestling in its
spacious valley. I finally arrived at a hamlet and took a side
road which led up past deserted farmhouses to an orchard.
Here I left the bike and climbed up a hill to a castle. I walked
up to the thick, splintered door and rapped on it. Thunk,
thunk! No answer, but I was suddenly startled by a blast of
wind which smashed the window shutters against the walls
and caused the sound to echo throughout the courtyard. It
could have been a protest of the past occupants at my unwel-
come intrusion. I walked through the garden, decayed and
sadly overgrown, with only the occasional marble column
or fountain to attest to the owners' former grandeur. I had
mixed feelings of sadness and joy as I walked through the
long grass and under the dark cypresses, a sadness from the
realization of human transience yet delight in the splendid
medievalness of the castle and the happy chatter of sparrows
further down the slopes. Dark winter day: "Fled is that
music. Do I wake or sleep?"

My trip up to Torre del Gallo reminded me that
Florence really does sit in a bowl in the foothills. The

Florentines refer to this bowl as a *conca* (literally conch). In Florentine dialect "conca" is pronounced "honca". To me it is a strange sounding dialect but I have no time to learn it. I have enough on my plate as it is!

Today was sunny with huge, billowy cumulous clouds, the grey Arno almost in flood proportions, and a brisk wind from the west. [25] After a lunch of several bowls of minestrone, Tuscan bread and a few glasses of wine I took a leisurely walk along the Arno, stopping to admire the fine jewelry, inspect the rebuilding of a bombed-out apartment, and have a look at Dante's house. Never have I seen the city more beautiful! The thought came to me that although my studies are important it is also important to do what I am doing right now: strolling around, observing, talking to the occasional person and drinking in the beauty of this incredibly beautiful city. Then I walked to the railroad station and priced tickets to Naples.

Gino's family lives in Torre Annunziata which lies on the Bay of Naples about fifteen miles south of Naples. Ah, these are the names that have bewitched me for the past few years: Almalfi, Capri, Ischia, Castellamare, Posilippo. Such names read like a little poem. I recall a bleak and rainy winter evening (typical Vancouver weather) last year at the university. I sat down with Tino (He's from Naples. Do you remember him?) in the student lounge and he hummed and explained to me each phrase (in Neapolitan dialect) of *Torna a Surriento*. What visions he conjured up for me! *Vedi Napoli poi muori!* See Naples and then die: *you might as well die because you've seen the most beautiful place on this planet.* I guess that's the idea behind those four little words. In any case, you can bet that I can't wait to see Sorrento for real!

I had to laugh the other night. The Colonel was telling us (Ede, Magda from Arezzo and me) about his conquests. He went on and on for what seemed like three hours. While listening I thought I heard the incongruous sound of heavy breathing. I looked around and there was Ede, sound asleep in her chair and snoring away! The colonel glanced at her in disbelief then spoke a few sharp words to her. She awoke with a start, at which the colonel grabbed his hat and cane and trotted off down the hall, shouting *"Avanti, Savoia!"* (I guess referring to King Vittorio Emmanuale, the king of Italy). It was an amusing performance.

I am glad to hear that you like Tebaldi. She's certainly my favorite soprano. Do you see Mike M at all? I have to laugh at his stupid racist remarks about Italians being inferior and non-Aryan. I think he does it to get a rise out of people. Even if his comments weren't malarky, he should be told that there is a great deal of nordic blood in Italy (Longobard and Celt in Northern Italy and Norman in Southern Italy.) I saw a busload of blond Sicilian tourists a few weeks ago up at Fiesole. Sicilian Vikings!

I had a great surprise the other day. I went into a bar just down the street and ordered an espresso. The barman, an old guy who looks quite Mafioso, looks at me with half-shut eyes and says, "Sure, buddy." Then he yells to the barman: "Hey, Enzo, shut that damn music up, will yuh?!" It turns out that I am addressing a Neapolitan who spent his youth in Brooklyn, then thirty years in Belgium, then ends up in Firenze. What an interesting world we live in! I am leaving for Naples and Torre Annunziata tomorrow morning.

January 12, 1961   Torre Annunziata

Dearest J,

Here I am in "Torre" and have been here for about a week now. With the temperature at about 65 degrees F. it feels like a warm April day in Vancouver. Imagine!—and it's early January. On my first day we started things off with a long walk along the beach. The sand is black and volcanic, which isn't surprising when you look around you. To the north and about fifteen miles away you can see the purple-green slopes of Vesuvius It is not that high, maybe four thousand feet (about the same elevation as Grouse Mountain in North Vancouver) but with altitude all similarity ends. Grouse Mountain is harmless; Vesuvius has a long record of causing nightmarish disasters. We passed an ancient wall on which the locals fought back the Saracens various times. (I couldn't get the dates.) It gives you a funny feeling to think of Arab hordes raiding this place in the name of Allah.

What a view we get from here! As you look out to sea: there's Sorrento on the far left, Capri straight out sea-ward and to your right, Naples, a vast area of white rising out of the sea. The sky is an unbelievable blue, almost robin's egg, nothing like our pale blue sky in the Pacific Northwest. Palm trees are everywhere. And I am getting my first glimpse of the Tyrrhenian Sea, the sea of Tyre —the Phoenicians.

126 *Florence, Dante and Me*

"Torre" itself is quite poor, but it's right on the ocean and they have made extensive gardens with lovely green palms for the use of citizens. The other day we went for a game of ping-pong in a hall which dates from about 1900. Photographs of King Umberto Emmanuele and his family dominated the room. I asked why they were there and was told that there are lots of royalists in Naples. It's apparently a kind of last stronghold. Maybe this goes back to their ties with the Bourbon kings—I'll have to read up on it. You can't help but think of Nelson and Lady Hamilton when you're in this area. I seem to recall that in an anti-royalist uprising Nelson gave military support to the Bourbon king. There's lots of poverty here but you'd never know it from the way people dress. All the men in the hall were dressed in suits, which says something about their pride in appearance, the old "bella figura" thing.

Naples as seen from the north

I sent you a postcard the other day and found out that postage on postcards is half price if your message is six words or less. Figure that one out.

Gino's family's house is white with very thick walls and has an almost adobe feel to it. Most of the living is done in one huge room which is dominated at one end by a huge bed and at the other end by a large grand piano. I didn't ask but I would guess that this piano was bought mostly for Gino's benefit and with considerable sacrifice on his parents' part.

The family consists of Gino's Dad (*Babbo* in Italian), his mother, Gino who is the eldest son, Enzo, a younger brother who is about eighteen, another brother about twelve, and a sister, Maria, who is about eight. She is a real charmer, bright, fun-loving and a bit coquettish. She asked me to read to her and ran to get the book: *Riccioli d'oro e i tre orsi* (Goldilocks and the Three Bears) which she thinks is absolutely the most. She is going to be a knockout when she gets older. The family speaks Italian to me but most of the time they speak Neapolitan, almost all of which escapes me. Gino clues me in whenever necessary.

The love shown for the *Mamma* in Gino's family is at times conscience-striking when I think of my own troubled relationship with my mother. At Gino's it's always "Mamma this" or "Mamma that" and a big kiss first thing every morning. As a guest of the eldest son, I'm waited on like a prince. "Can I take your coat?" "Please sit here." "Do eat." "Don't dwell on ceremony!" "Don't wait for us!" At every meal a huge pot of pasta is placed on the table and everyone digs in without ceremony. I eat this wonderful pasta until I'm gorged, then there's salad, fish, sea-shells of some kind, fruit, nuts and wine. And you mustn't say "grazie" for anything or you get *Ma che grazie!?* (said with a furrowed brow and a look of consternation). *Mangia,* (Eat), *Roberto. Mangia! Non ti preoccupare!* (Don't worry!). *Assaggia un po di questo!*

(Try a little of this!). I look at them pleadingly, in friendly dismay. It gets more complicated. Me (in Italian): "A thousand thanks, but I absolutely can't eat any more!" When they question this protest, even they have to laugh at my clincher: *Scusi, proprio non ne sono capace.* I am not physically capable of it (i.e. eating any more)! Then I say to them *Voi non siete Italiani, ma Napoletani!* (You are not Italians, you're Neapolitans!) This is greeted with gales of laughter and nodding heads. They consider this kind of hospitality their duty: *Il nostro dovere.*

Maria's mother

Maria

We eat like royalty, and this in spite of what seems to me poverty (Maybe I'm wrong.) All the walls are cracked and there is no indoor plumbing. I guess we're spoiled in Canada.

You say you despise Christianity but isn't forgiveness at the core of Christianity and isn't forgiveness a very, very beautiful thing? I wish there had been more of it in my family. I am thinking of Gino's mother now and how the family treats her. If my mother had forgiven my grandmother maybe she would never have swept her aside into an old folk's home. She would have taken her in and we all would have looked after her. And if my mother had forgiven my biological father (a very hard thing to do because he had beaten her viciously) she probably would not have taken out on me (in subtle ways) the revenge that she harbored for him. Anyway, we have lots to learn from these Neapolitans and the kind way they treat their old people. Not that it's all peaches and cream here. A couple of times Gino has made fun of his father's lack of education, making cracks like "Oh, just like when you were in university, eh?" I don't know why he does this but it seems like a cruel jab because his father had only a couple of years of schooling, never mind the conservatory! On the other hand, I don't know the whole picture; maybe Gino has good reasons.

As I was saying, there is a huge grand piano in the middle of the living room. I am sure that the piano was bought to help Gino pursue his career as a professional musician (specializing in violin) and I bet his parents sacrificed a lot to buy that piano. He plays it well (he had to take piano too at the conservatory) and the other day he sat down and attempted to compose a popular song. I watched him as he plunked out phrases. If he thinks up something good he could make a lot of money. I would like to see him compose something in the romantic style of Peppino di Capri who is such a hit over here. Is he at all known in Canada? I doubt it.

This morning I watched Gino's grandmother make pasta. She is old but she's still a handsome woman and her forearms are sinewy and strong-looking. The pasta dough is first mixed with water then rolled out in snake-shaped strips which are in turn chopped into one-half inch pieces, then rolled and bent into shell-like shapes. This lady is honored in the family and seeing how she is treated makes me sad to think of my own grandmother living alone for many years in a dreary bedsitter in a West

Vancouver nursing home. It's a shame that my mother never let go of the grudge she held against her for not supporting her in the divorce litigation against my biological father. Anyway, we have lots to learn from these Neapolitans and the way they look after their old folks. **[26]**

On Sunday Gino and I visited Pompeii with Franco whose father had an important part to play in recent excavations. It was a splendid day: sunny, with just a little morning haze. I am impressed with the richness of the crops that spring from the black volcanic soil, even in January.

Pompeii is vast and has been excavated with amazing success. I jotted down notes to remind myself: before the eruption Pompeii was a port but during the eruption much of the land heaved up so it became an inland city, two miles from the ocean and well above it in altitude. The walls of the buildings are dark and somber, often with jagged tops. In contrast, the grass (where there is any) is lush and very green. This place is unlike any I have ever seen. It has an eerie, tragic atmosphere. The buildings are very ancient yet somehow they look surprisingly modern. I saw several petrified forms. One contained three men and a dog, contorted and agonizing. I saw combs, a round grain-grinder, egg shells, bread, and nuts (scorched but intact). I also saw fine gold coins of beautiful workmanship. Maybe the most intriguing thing I saw was a large gold-colored safety pin. I couldn't believe what I was looking at: a safety pin, exactly like the ones we use nowadays. I had always assumed that they were a modern invention. Now I am willing to believe almost anything about what they had in ancient Rome.

It took us the best part of a morning to walk through Pompeii quickly. Franco explained things of interest: *Tempio del genio di Augusto,* (Temple of the patron spirit of Augustus); the market street; the tragic and comic theaters; the gladiator pits; the house of two rich merchants (complete with a private brothel). The public baths are extensive and include both Roman and Turkish types. The streets are paved with huge stones and you can see the grooves worn in them over the centuries by chariot wheels. I kept half expecting to see Charlton Heston (Ben Hur) careening around the corner in a chariot! You get a real idea of ancient Rome in this place. The many small objects of everyday life make you wonder: Who owned this? What were they like?

Pompeii more or less as it was in 1961

After Pompeii we visited New Pompeii to see the Church of the Madonna of the Miracle. She has performed many miracles, they say, and I see no reason to doubt it. [27] You know, in freshman year at UBC I filled out a questionnaire and said that I was an atheist. I thought I was so smart and hip. I no longer feel this way. I think I might be going through some kind of conversion but I am not sure how to explain it. Maybe the spirituality of the things I've seen and experienced in Italy has moved my heart and mind: Saint Francis of Assisi, Dante, Giotto, Michelangelo. I would even add Signor Rotelli (the consul in Vancouver), Signora Bianchi, Ede Parenti and Colonel Cugiani. The list is long.

Yesterday Enzo and I went to Castellamare (about seven miles to the south of Torre, still on Bay of Naples) to see the sun set over Capri. We climbed the steep hill behind the town to see it. It was magnificent. Funny how the view westwards reminded me of Horseshoe Bay in West Vancouver.

I am starting to understand a bit of the *Napoletano* dialect but most of it still escapes me. If normal speech in English is clear, simple and unemotional, normal speech in Italian is quite different. Many Italians I've met don't shy away from scholarly words and dramatic, emotional language: *Ecco il Canadese!* (Behold the Canadian!). *Io capisco tutto a volo!* (I understand everything on the fly!) Such phrases must be declaimed dramatically, almost defiantly. I find myself copying them. I'm going to sound pretty weird if I carry over this habit into English!

Do you think you tend to scorn slang and colloquialisms? I think there is a place for them although the university seems to encourage us to frown on them, making linguistic snobs of us in the process. I much prefer "somewhat" to "rather"—you hear nothing but "rather" among English majors. You also hear affected sounding expressions like "I should have thought that", "We could posit that" and a crazy tendency to see "dichotomies" everywhere. I think it's the old Canadian tendency to ape the upper class English.

I was quite amused by the description of me by one of the professors to whom you've been passing my letters: *"a naturally adventurous character enhanced by a modicum of conservativeness."* Typical language of an academic! I love it! I don't see myself as very conservative but maybe I am. Anyhow, I guess I should take his remark as a compliment. "Adventurous" is a nice thing to be called. By the way, please forward some of my letters to my parents. I don't have time to write them much. I am glad you are editing the letters before making a typed copy.

Florence, Dante and Me

I just finished lunch with Gino and his family. They forced me to eat five large ladles of spaghetti with Neapolitan beans (very flavorful). After the spaghetti we had fried herrings and salad. I think I amused them by eating a fish head and fibbing that in Canada we eat the head of giant salmon. Right now, just outside my door, an old lady is washing clothes by hand and singing a dirge-like song. Very mysterious.

Statue of an Elvis look-alike in
the Museo Nazionale, Naples

The other day I visited the National Museum in Naples with Gino. It has a fabulous collection of Greek marble statues and I almost swooned in the room of Venuses. They seem to have assembled under one roof the best sculpture of ancient Greece. It's an incredible collection. I had never felt that much touched by the beauty of sculpture but having seen these Greek statues all that has changed. I have been converted. You won't believe this, but I almost fell over backwards when I saw a statue of a handsome young man with a trim swimmer's build, a Roman nose and a slightly curled lip. He was the spitting image of Elvis Presley! Face it, you goodie-two-shoes, Pat Boone-loving, Eagle scout, Elvis-haters, Presley is damned good looking! I think this is the most amazing, most surprising thing that I have ever seen.

Enzo

I had to laugh at Gino's younger brother, Enzo. We went shopping for dress shoes in Naples. (Wide selection and incredibly low prices. All pointed toes, I tell you.) I see a pair I like and Enzo handles the transaction in dialect. He bargains a 500 lira (approximately 80 cents) discount for me and the shoes are put in a bag. We start walking out and Enzo turns suddenly to the salesman and gives him a 500 lira tip. When I ask Enzo what's happening he just protrudes his lips, raises his hands while shrugging his shoulders, looks straight ahead and says, *Che vuoi?* (What do you expect?) Hoo ha! In the late afternoon we took a stroll along the waterfront near Santa Lucia. We stopped and watched an old fisherman bucket and clean his catch. I guess his ancestors have been doing this for many centuries. I didn't feel the temperature of the ocean but I hear you can swim all year long off the island of Ischia in the Bay of Naples.

Naples has many new light-colored apartment houses. This reinforces the overall impression you get of the place: a great white city, very ancient, set on a remarkably beautiful bay. What impresses me is the life in the streets, the hundreds of little urchins, and the colors of the market. I have heard that there is a huge black market here and a mafia-like organization called the *Camorra* so maybe there is a whole dark side to this city that I know absolutely nothing about. **[28]** The people here are fairly short and it is good to have the feeling that (at five feet nine) I am suddenly tall, almost a giant! From time to time I feel stared at or maybe I should say closely observed. They might be staring at my *pizzo* (goatee) or the tartan vest which I often wear. Maybe they think that I just stepped out of a production of *Lucia di Lammermoor* with my Scottish-Celtic look. I like to think so.

I realize that I've got into the expensive habit of traveling a lot by train. I've already spent a week's portion of next month's cheque. Italy (and Europe) are much bigger than I thought. At least I have pretty well confined my train travel to Italy. I am interested in seeing northern Europe but I find myself drawn overwhelmingly to countries which touch on the Mediterranean and whose language has been inherited from the Romans: Italy, France and Spain.

The other evening there was a knock on the door. A lady neighbor invited Gino, Enzo and me to a party. We went immediately. Gino and I both like dancing so we invited two girls to dance and that really seemed to get the party moving. When we were leaving an elderly woman said to me (in *Napoletano*) that "we'd brought the sun with us." A beautiful thing to say, isn't it? And to me it seems typical of the Neapolitans. They are born poets and able to express emotions with images taken from nature: the sun, the rain, a tempest, a shower, a rainbow. At this same party I was introduced to a guy about fifty who had spent ten years in America. He spoke Neapolitan but absolutely no English (or he didn't let on, if he could!) or even standard Italian. Weird. I guess he was incapable of being transplanted. I wonder how many Italians emigrated to the USA but after living there a while returned to Italy for good.

Later that same evening when I was in bed I heard some loud frenzied music in the street below my window. I flung open the wooden shutters and gaped out to see about a dozen people dancing frantically in the dark street below. "Unbelievable!" I thought. "Oh, well," I muttered as I went back to bed, "They're Napoletani!" Then it occurred to me, "Of course, it figures! This is where the *tarantella* was invented!"

On my last night in Naples I walked alone through Torre. It seemed like spring was in the air with a warm wind off the ocean, crashing breakers and Mediterranean palms. This is a special part of the planet.

Pinching bottoms, you say? I don't know where you got this but I have been here for six months now and I have not seen one person pinch anyone's backside.

On my final day at Gino's I took leave of the family. Mr. A. made a nice speech telling me how glad they were to have me stay with them. When I tried to express my thanks, he protested so I shut up. I didn't want to receive "the furrowed brow look". What charming people! I am sure we will always be friends. How I wish I could have talked to them in that dramatic, musical dialect of theirs. They insisted that I take with me on the train a hollowed-out loaf of bread stuffed with herrings. As if I hadn't had enough to eat! I plan to stop in Rome for a few days before going back to Florence.

January 15, 1961   Rome

Dearest J,

I have just spent three days in Rome and decided to write
you now that my impressions are still pretty clear. I visited
the Vatican again (I had seen only a small part of it on my
last visit.) I spent five hours in the Vatican Museum which
contains an endless succession of galleries. It's amazingly
lavish. Highlights for me were Botticelli's sketches for *La
Divina Commedia* and a sixteenth century copy of Dante's
book with lovely colored plates; Raphael's apartments with
his magnificent painting of the philosophers of Athens; the
Sistine Chapel with its remarkable *Giudizio Universale* (I
wish I had thought to bring binoculars to get a clear view
of the frescoes on the ceiling.); and the Etruscan-Egyptian
Museum in which I saw a ghastly mummy with hair, teeth
and fingernails all intact. There were swarms of people in
the Sistine but the other rooms were not very crowded. I
overheard one tourist say to another: "Come on, Mable,
let's get out of here!" It made me wonder what had possessed her to visit the Sistine in the first place.

   Yesterday I wandered around the Forum and saw
some interesting things. If you stand in the Forum and
look towards the Capitoline Hill you can see a cliff about
fifty feet high. It's called *la rupe Tarpea* and it was used
to execute certain types of undesirables: traitors first and
foremost but also slaves who were caught stealing. The
ancient Romans were not people to trifle with.

La Rupe Tarpea (The Tarpean cliff)

I had to laugh today. I'm walking along the street near the Forum and wondering what time it is. I see a priest coming down the street towards me in his black robes and round, broad-brimmed hat. He looks dapper and maybe a bit effeminate. *Scusi, Padre. Che ore sono?* (What time is it?), says I. He, not having heard clearly, leans over me and in an almost conspiratorial way whispers: *Dica tutto!* (Tell me everything!) When I repeat *Che ore sono?* his face suddenly clouds over with disappointment and he replies theatrically and with mock incredulity: *Non c'è altro que quello?!* (Isn't there something else apart from that i.e. What time is it?). These Italians, I tell you! I also had a good chat with a guy in a used book shop who had fought the Russians on the Eastern Front. He was convinced that they, the Italians and Germans, should have won.

I spent a few hours in the Castel Sant'Angelo, where I particularly enjoyed the fifteenth century jailer's quarters. What came to mind was the last act of *Tosca* in which Mario Cavaradossi bribes the jailer with his family ring in exchange for pen and paper so that he can write a farewell letter to his beloved Tosca.

> Unico resto di mia richezza è questo anel.
> *The only remaining thing of my riches is this ring.*
>
> Se promettete di consegnarle il mio ultimo addio esso è vostro!
> *If you promise to deliver to her my last farewell it is yours!*

I also thought of that brave fellow, Benvenuto Cellini, who managed to escape from this prison by jumping off the parapet. The castle houses showcases which show the development of arms and armor from the fourteenth to the eighteenth century. I found them fascinating. The view from the top of the castle is a noble one. [See photo in the March 15th letter.]

I spent a few hours with Jaqub, my Jordanian friend from the University of Perugia. We shared the fried herrings stuffed in a hollowed-out loaf of bread which Mr. A. had insisted I take with me on the train. Jaqub, whose native language is Arabic, is studying medicine at the University of Rome. All of his courses are in Italian. I admire his courage.

Here in Italy (and in my brief visit to Switzerland) I've become aware of the importance which educated people attach to learning at least one, and preferably two, foreign languages. When I lived in Vancouver I had heard that this was so but it was only an impression, a vague awareness based on no experience. Now I know that it's a fact.

January 28, 1961   Florence, Via dei Serragli

Dear J,

What's happening? I haven't heard from you for two weeks now! **[29]**

I am sitting here freezing because my gas burner's out. *Porca miseria!* (Swinish poverty!) Thanks for the parcel. What taste and imagination you have: Shakespeare's sonnets, poems by Dylan Thomas, a jar of strawberry jam and a pipe. The pipe suits me well. I will really look like a Scot or a Limey when I walk through the streets now, what with the beard, a jacket with leather patches at the elbows, a tartan vest and a pipe. It's a lovely Christmas package and it's not your fault if it took over a month to get here. Speaking of beards, mine has been commented on. I was sitting in a barber shop and waiting my turn when I heard one of the barbers use the phrase *il signore con il pizzo.* I knew he was referring to me but I didn't let on. I find it's sometimes wise to pretend you don't understand because that's when you hear things that you aren't meant to hear. I am not sure what Italians think of *pizzi.* I don't see many men with them. Mussolini was against beards and there might be some anti-beard attitudes lingering on. I sense in some people that they still have a soft spot for *Il Duce.*

Today I sent off a few postcards to Canada, including one to my old high school principal, James Inkster of West

Van High. **[30]** I am hoping to see *Hiroshima, Mon Amour* but it hasn't come here yet.

I will have my first singing lesson with a Signora Del Vivo next week. Ha! I shall finally find out if I have a voice or the potential to develop one. I will keep you posted.

I have met through landlady Ede an excellent tailor by the name of Signor Annichini. I visited him in his apartment to see samples of his work. It is top notch and I am confident that he will do a fine job. He is obviously a master tailor and his suits are on the level of Saville Row. I have decided to order a made to measure three piece suit and a winter coat. The suit will cost me $75. and the coat will cost $50. These prices are amazing. I can't imagine what they would cost in Canada but even if I did have them made in Canada I doubt if I could find a tailor of Annichini's caliber. I chose the materials today and had my measurements taken. The wool is soft and the colors so rich: dark brown for the suit and a kind of loden green for the winter coat. I think he said the cloth is by Cerruti which is apparently the best you can get. I felt it and I'm sure he's right. I will be dressed like a prince! **[31]**

I am back into a daily routine: classes at the university, lunch at my *trattoria,* studying at the Marucelliana library, a visit to a museum, or coffee with someone. I am going to a public reading of Dante tomorrow night in the *Via dell'arte della lana* (The Street of the Wool Art). How medieval, eh? And it ties right in with my visits to the tailor, Signor Annichini.

It's now midnight and I was just forced to pour a large glass of water out the window and onto the head of some crumb in the street who was making excessive noise with a motorcycle. Unfortunately I missed. Maybe I need practice!

Sometimes I think that four years in a row at UBC would have been a little much. Maybe I'm rationalizing because I am disappointed that I might be "losing a year". Yes, "losing a year", and yet I've learned so much and I've gained the experience of a lifetime. How stupid it is to fear falling behind in the crazy race to get a B.A. in four years! What a stupid materialistic-competitive outlook I've allowed myself to buy into! I am trying to think along different lines. Seeing how people live in Italy has changed me in other ways too. I started to feel some compassion (and guilt) when I saw a little old lady staggering along with a heavy basket of clothes on her head or when I saw the laundrywoman at work at six a.m. and then when I returned that evening at nine p.m. found her still working. I used to think that I could be a student forever, travel around Europe and drink wine and eat pasta. I don't think that kind of life is morally justified. A university bum, I now think, is one of the most contemptible, useless specimens in our society. Here I have seen lots of people (not students) working hard for forty hours a week and earning only two or three dollars a day. This has made me see that it's my duty to study hard, get qualified, and then contribute something to society, probably as a teacher or professor. Society has a long way to go in making sure that everyone who works receives a decent wage. There's a lot of unfairness in the world.

I am still not sure about the summer. I am honor-bound by the scholarship to remain here until mid-June. Summer jobs are very scarce in Vancouver. There's no guarantee I'll get one so I am tempted to spend the summer in France, especially since it looks more and more like I will be making French and Italian literature my career. (I don't like this word "career"—it's more like a passionate interest.) Maybe I can find some kind of summer job in France. There's certainly lots I want to see there. I am looking forward to having a close look at the Louvre because they have works by some of my favorite painters. Another possibility would be to take two upper division courses in French literature at UBC. Much would depend on what is offered and who is teaching.

February 5, 1961   Florence

Dear J,

It's Sunday today, and the sky is a deep azure, a blue such
as I have never seen in Canada. It's not spring, but spring is
in the air. The breeze is not so cold and I hear the warbling
of a few early chirpers in the morning. I guess they have
just returned from Africa or Malta.

Ah, bel canto!—that lovely ringing style that gives
every note exceptional purity, tone and naturalness, the
style that makes the Italians the best singers in the world,
the style that enabled Caruso to shatter a wine glass with
a high C and enables Maria Callas to cause shivers in the
remotest gallery at La Scala. You guessed it: I have started
my singing lessons. Finally! I already see the posters: *Tosca*
at La Scala. Scarpia: Roberto Tommassini. God, I'd sacrifice university to be a singer! Any day! My *maestra di canto*
is Signora Nedda Del Vivo and it was Signor Annichini
(the tailor) who put me on to her. She lives a three mile bike
ride from my place, north of the Arno, out near the soccer
stadium. Her studio is on the second floor of a newish
apartment. I have five months to study with her: one hour
twice a week at 1000 lire an hour. This hurts my budget
but she is good, very good. I sensed it right away. I am
lucky to have found her. I might have to find more private
students in order to pay her.

This woman is amazing at the keyboard. She changes keys in the twinkling of an eye and without even looking at the keyboard. As she plays she just continues to look at you fixedly in the eye and you wonder: *"Ma cosa le sta passando per la testa?!"* (What is going through that head of hers?) Her playing is so artistically phrased that she makes the exercises sound like little rhapsodies. This is an artist! By the way, I had a second fitting for my suit and coat with Signor Annichini and they are looking like works of art as well. More and more Florence seems to me a city of artists.

Signora Nedda del Vivo

The other day I took a walk in the Boboli Gardens, had lunch and then took in a symphony concert in the magnificent Hall of the Five Hundred in the Palazzo Vecchio. Greek statues of Hercules' labors line the perimeter and the walls have frescoes by Vasari of great battles in Florentine history. They play Beethoven's Seventh. (Oh, those French horns in the last movement!) Then they play Wagner's *Götterdämmerung*, which is very grandiose and inspiring in certain passages. I'm inclined to think Beethoven "the King of Music": technically and inspirationally he seems perfect. To think that he composed while deaf is incredible. The man seems superhuman or divinely inspired.

I have stopped reading Mme de Stael. Her style and ideas are monotonous. I see no point to reading second rate authors when I could be reading the best: Dante, Shakespeare, Molière, etc.

The trouble is that the universities make it mandatory to study second rate authors.

Some Italian customs are *molto curiose*. No decent woman would be caught dead smoking in the street, but smoking while she's dancing with you, or smoking in the cinema, now that's a different matter! At the university library almost all of the books can be kept out indefinitely. And who'd even think of a fine? God, that would be restricting one's liberty! *Viva la liberta!!* Maybe the Latin mentality is liberty-crazy (or maybe we Anglo-Saxons have been spoiled by having enjoyed it for so long). What a difference from Canadian libraries! Movies: I went to see Camus' *Rio Negro* the other day. It was good, but not as powerful as the *Black Orpheus* which we saw last year in Vancouver.

The author and the statue of Hercules and Cacus, Piazza della
Signoria, Florence.

February 15, 1961   Florence

Dearest J,

It's two a.m. and I have just been awakened by some drunks singing at full blast in the street. There are lots of drunks in my *quartiere*. They got the sudden downpour.

On a more positive note, the singing lessons are going very well. This is the real *bel canto* method and it seems to have as much to do with mental attitudes as it does with producing notes. We use deep diaphragmic breathing and I breathe through the nose. The idea is to get to feel that I am producing the sound from somewhere up near my eyes and to get the sound up there I start by humming. Early in the lessons we figured out with the piano where my good notes lie. My best note is the F an octave and a half below middle C. We start from this low F and go up: F-G-A then down G-F then up again (G-A), and so on, three times, finishing on a whole note. I crescendo going up and diminuendo coming down. Great care is taken to keep the color of the notes consistent. We do this over and over and over! And faster and faster. Any bad phrasing or incorrect dynamics or flat or sharp note is brought to my attention, let me tell you. Exercises and more exercises. *Niente canzoni!* (Absolutely no songs!) the Maestra says. Not for months! It seems that my voice has some (six, to be precise) really good notes so this is where we are doing our work, repeating the exercises until the notes become fuller and richer. When my notes are right I can feel and hear a kind of buzzing sound. We will gradually extend the range, both upwards and downwards, from this cluster of good notes. The cluster becomes stronger and stronger so that when I reach the top note I feel the energy and champ at the bit to increase the range. There is no forcing things on my part. Finally! I think I will be able to get higher notes without straining and hurting my throat. This has always been a problem when I sing.

As I walked along the Lungarno the other day it was crowded with elegant Florentines in their Sunday best. Children in carnival costumes, yelling, blowing horns and throwing confetti. A little man was selling balloons. He resembled Charlie Chaplin and looked very much in danger of being swept away by his great bunch of balloons, over the parapet and into the Arno. I could see a few fishermen basking in the sun, maybe smiling at the clever excuse they used to get away from their Signora for the day, and small groups of British sailors, some tattooed and bearded, with bell-bottoms and sparkling white caps.

Don't take too seriously that paragraph I wrote on being disillusioned with the romantic aspects of Italy. I was in a down mood. On days like today I find that here there's more life, color and romance (plus the thrilling sense of history and of centuries past) than you could hope to find in western Canada. Many times I have felt this and overall I am definitely not homesick for Vancouver although at the moment I have to admit that I'd give anything for a plate of waffles with butter and Maple syrup. They don't seem to have them over here (Hey, that might be a money-making business to set up!) Too bad you didn't join me for my year over here because you have missed a great deal. I think a young, sensitive, romantic person would get far more 'food for the soul' from just living in Europe than the most scholarly, learned person would get from her galleries, monuments and architecture.

The book I recommended on Michelangelo is by Ludwig Goldscheider. Many of the plates show Michelangelo's unfinished works. He was never satisfied with them. This I find very disconcerting. The church of San Lorenzo is full of Michelangelo's spirit. This is where you can see his sculptures *La Notte*, *L'aurora*, etc. that are placed on the tombs of the Medici.

February 21, 1961   Florence

Carissima J,

It's ten p.m. and I am writing this from my room overlooking the wine-drinking joint across the *vicolo*. It's quite cosy
here. Ede has provided me with a furry goatskin to keep my
feet warm while I study. Very nice of her. Anyway, as I was
saying, the wine drinkers are really in their cups tonight
and having a merry time but for the past few minutes I can
hear the language degenerating. One guy has just shouted
at someone that he is a *vigliacco* (a coward) and things will
probably escalate because this is a fighting word. Tuning
in on situations like this is interesting and a good way to
get the sense of what some words really mean.

   This evening I went to the Linguists' Club and got
chatting with a very Victorian English colonel. This was
a treat. He must have felt uncomfortable because I was
always smiling and laughing, not so much at his few dry
jests, but at him! After all, there he was, wearing a mon-
ocle on a string around his neck and talking about doing
exercises every morning at eighty years of age. He knew
precisely how many steps (89) lead up to his apartment!

   The singing lesson went well today and my voice is
now anchored somewhere between the eyes. It's nice of you
to call me "Caruso II" and it fits because I fell in love with
opera by watching Mario Lanza play Caruso in *The Great
Caruso* (1951). I was only eleven but I was hooked, and I

mean hooked! But you should call me "George London II" because I am a bass-baritone too and besides, both London and I are from Vancouver! London is one of the best in the business. His Don Giovanni is superb! Maestra Del Vivo doesn't think I've the voice for Verdi but she thinks maybe I can do Mozart.

At the university I'm doing six hours per week on very difficult translations: French to Italian and vice versa. I've a paper to do for Monday (in French) on an intriguing statement by Lamartine: *"La poésie chante bien, pleure bien, mais décrit mal."* (Poetry sings well, weeps well, but describes badly.) A nasty little assignment. I am still reading Dante on my own. There hasn't been much opera here because the Communale Opera house has been undergoing renovations since November. I am looking forward to the famous Florentine music festival in May, the *Maggio Musicale Fiorentino* (musical little phrase, is it not?).

I've been doing a lot of reading in the *Enciclopedia italiana,* (The Italian is very advanced, maybe more than you'd expect) just to get information on things that interest me: Bronzino, Castiglione, Paul Verlaine. What are their major works? What was their life like? I take notes and this helps me to place whatever work of art I see in the museums, churches, etc. I was reading recently that Michelangelo got into a fight with Pietro Torrigiano when he was a student in Ghirlandaio's workshop and got his nose broken ('totally smashed in' is more like it). These are things not mentioned in guide books. The broken nose episode would explain a lot about Michelangelo: his anger, his tendency to quarrel, his misanthropic tendencies. By the way, I'm glad you like the recording [of French-Canadian music] that I recommended. The song I like best is *Au Bois du Rossignolet*. It makes me think of Quebec: flying loons and *seigneuries* sloping down to a vast, grey St. Lawrence River, hardy French-Canadian loggers riding the logs down the Ottawa, brave Dollard des Ormeaux and his small band of men fighting off the Iroquois, and so on. I envy French-Canadians their history which seems so much more colorful than ours. To quote their version of our anthem: *Ton histoire est une épopée des plus brillants exploits*. (Your history is an epic poem of the most brilliant exploits.) They are referring to Dollard, Radisson, Madeleine de Verchères, heroes of that kind.). How pale and insipid is our version in English: "And we stand on guard, oh, Canada, we stand on guard for thee!"

February 27, 1961   Florence

My dear J,

We are in the middle of carnival here and I have been down with the Asiatic flu. Rats! In the bars and pastry stores some remarkable cakes have suddenly appeared. It seems to be all part of carnival. Speaking of food, Ede and Tosca invited me for lunch last Sunday. They both cooked. Some meal! Two plate-loads of lasagna; roast chicken, roast potatoes and roast artichokes (from Sicily); several glasses of Orvieto wine; for dessert: pastries with whipped cream, liqueurs and fruit. Carlo Buti provided the entertainment.

I have been doing all kinds of reading and came across a quotation from Dickens' *Pictures from Italy* (which I thought you'd like):

> "But how much beauty of another kind is here, when on a fair clear morning, we look from the summit of a hill, on Florence! See where it lies before us in a sun-lighted valley, bright with the winding Arno, and shut in by swelling hills, its domes and towers and palaces rising from the glittering country in a glittering heap, and shining in the sun like gold."

One of the fascinating things about living in Florence is the ghosts of the great foreign artists who have lived here. The Brownings lived in Casa Guidi, just a few streets over.

Looking down from the side of Brunelleschi's cathedral

Their apartment has been preserved with all the original furniture and you step into their cosy little love nest just as it was. It's not hard to imagine them present. Elizabeth Barrett-Browning had this to say: "What Florence is, the tongue of man or poet may easily fail to describe. The most beautiful of cities, with the golden Arno shot through the breast of her like an arrow, and "non dolet" all the same." It's hard to imagine an arrow not causing pain but that's a poet for you! As you stand in the street outside the Brownings' residence you see another plaque (*in italiano*) indicating the residence of another great writer who spent time here: "In this room the great Russian novelist Dostoievsky finished his novel *The Idiot*". Bits of knowledge like this really bring home to you how cosmopolitan and widely loved this city has been. It's always a thrill to come across these plaques. Dozens of them refer to people and places in *The Divine Comedy* too. By the way (and I hesitate to mention this), I have the distinct impression at times that the little room I live in is haunted. I sense a presence and I hear things. I wonder if it's Dante Parenti.

I look upon this year as one that has civilized or 'culturalized' me first hand. Something I'll miss of Florence are the tawny, rabbit-eared, stubborn donkeys that tug huge carts of twigs through the streets, heedless of the scowling, branch-snapping *padrone* seated on his cart. Also the elegant nineteenth century *carrozze* pulled by stately chestnut-colored horses, clattering over the cobbles, while their occupants, two blonde American girls, look around with a sophisticated air.

The leather book covers here are lovely (and cheap: eighty cents and up). If you have a couple of books you'd like covers for, send me the dimensions. The Florentines seem to be great craftsmen in just about anything they put their hand to. I am thinking about buying a second hand scooter but I don't know if I can raise the money. **[32]**

I think that you hadn't thought of Sinatra as being "great" because he sings popular songs. Over here Sinatra and Crosby are considered great artists in the *classico-popolare* genre or what we would call popular standards. I think this is because they have rich, warm voices and technical perfection of delivery—breath control. Sinatra's breath control is phenomenal and it enables him to join seamlessly long, high phrases in the way Tommy Dorsey does on the trombone. I think you grossly underestimate Frank Sinatra as an artist. I see him as without equal in the blues of a reverie kind (*Ebb Tide, I'm a Fool to Want You, All or nothing at all, The Gal that got away*, etc.) Maybe his "popularity" puts you off and you think that his wide accessibility excludes him from the ranks of great artists. I don't think this kind of criticism makes much sense. Isn't it the same kind of snobbish attitude that makes some people scorn to put Puccini (who is so accessible) in the same league as Bach and Wagner?

By living over here I am discovering singers that I would never have found out about if I had stayed in Canada. Mina, who won the San Remo song festival this year, is an example. Her big hit is *Cielo in Una Stanza di Notte* (Sky in a room at night): *Quando*  *tu sei vicina a me, questa stanza non ha più pareti ma alberi, alberi infiniti...* (When you are near me this room doesn't have walls any more but trees, infinite trees.) She sings with typical Italian passion and imagination! However, she is not even close to being in the league of an Ella Fitzgerald or Peggy Lee. In the world of popular singing the Americans rule and I know of no popular singers from Europe who would cause me to change my mind.

Quite popular over here is Nat King Cole and his *Chiquita*.

I saw the eclipse the other morning. We were plunged into total night for a couple of minutes. It gave me the shivers and I found myself thinking of the *Dies Irae* and the great chorus from Verdi came rushing through my brain. At 8:37 a.m. my bridge, the *Ponte alla Carraia*, was packed with people. School kids with their books; stooped, wooly-capped little old men pausing with their push-carts; the knife and scissors grinder pausing on his ungainly grindstone-bearing bike; businessmen, beautifully-suited, smugly observing the phenomenon through pieces of shaded glass; the mysterious little fruit-vendor or whatever he is who wakes me up at 9:00 every other morning raucously yelling strange, incomprehensible words that sound like "Take care of me!", that echo in the *vicolo*.

I have had yet another fitting of my new suit. It's a knockout! Annichini is a perfectionist, like Michelangelo. Also, I have just learned that one of my favorite tenors, Mario del Monaco, is a Fiorentino. I'm not surprised. Maestra Del Vivo told me a fascinating story about her youth. She lived in the country and wasn't allowed to practice singing in her parents' house so she explored a bit and found herself a cave—a very damp, and not too pleasant one, I gather—and practiced her *vocalizi* there. I guess the acoustics would have been great.

March 4, 1961

Hi, J, lots of good happenings here,

I've mistaken professions! The singing lessons are going
great! Boy, am I enthusiastic! What is frustrating is that
I am allowed to sing only at my lessons, not at home. I
guess the idea is that I might ruin my voice or pick up bad
habits if I try stuff on my own. If my voice develops as I
hope it will, she assures me that I will be a *cannonata* (a
big success). She is thinking of negro spirituals (and I am
thinking of *Porgy and Bess*). I'm willing and hoping! Music
has always been my major interest, maybe even more than
literature, but I have never suspected all that much apti-
tude (apart from an excellent memory for tunes). This
raises a problem about coming home in June. I should
remain here for the summer and continue with the lessons
to make sure that I never lose what I have acquired here.
Maestra Del Vivo is not sure if I can develop the power
necessary for grand opera. She thinks maybe Mozart.
Well, we shall see. You never quite know what this bel
canto stuff is going to find in your throat! Anyway, for
the next five months it's all scales and exercises. She also
suggests I learn enough with her so that I won't need a
teacher in Vancouver. The idea is for me to study on my
own. This would mean getting a piano to work with. The
good thing is that once the voice is developed, it never
leaves you. Even if I never sing professionally it will give

me great pleasure to be able to use my voice to its best advantage in the years to come.

I have become good friends with my professor of French literature at the university. He calls for my opinion quite often in class and addresses me (with slightly ironic intonation) as "le monsieur du Nouveau Monde" or "Monsieur le Canadien". Dr. Halbwachs is his name. He is Jewish and a victim of Auschwitz. How he managed to keep his marbles (and even his humor) after that nightmare is really amazing. His analyses, especially of Balzac and Baudelaire, are superb and a model for me to copy. We analyzed a passage from Balzac about the morning wake up routine of a cat in the pension Vauquier. Some of the words even sound like a cat. What an amazing writer! Halbwachs and I have good chats as we sometimes walk together all the way from the university in Piazza San Marco to the Palazzo Pitti area (a mile and a half). He advises me on things to read and has loaned me books, e. g. *Causeries de Lundi* by a brilliant French critic, Sainte Beuve. Halbwachs is here on a kind of exchange. He started out on the wrong foot in the course by conducting the class in faltering Italian. I was the ringleader in getting several students together to convince him to lecture in French. Thank heaven he was reasonable and saw the light! Funny that he tried to pull a fast one like this. At the moment we are reading Alfred de Musset's *Lorenzaccio*. I am not keen on it. Halbwachs mentions current events from time to time, making sure we don't get stuck in the nineteenth century. He brought up Gagarin's amazing flight through space the other day. What's next? The moon?

I received a letter from the Italian Government two days ago saying that my scholarship is not renewable and ends this June. This puts a different light on things. I shall really have to take advantage of the time remaining. I am pleased with the way my understanding of French and Italian has progressed. My work on Italian-French translations has helped. The big advantage to translation work is that there is no room for thinking in English. English somehow gets squeezed out in the translation process and one's mind in not operating in an English sphere.

Big news: I am planning to move to a quieter part of town. This is no place for an insomniac and my insomnia is so bad that I don't even try to go to bed before one a.m. Magda's shouting, the drunks in front of the *vinaio* in the street below—both have been really getting to me lately. Not even the *camomilla* tea that Ede introduced me to could solve the problem. I shall be really sorry to leave the "family" here: Ede, Gino and the Colonel. These people have shown me great kindness and we have shared meals, jokes, poems, songs, movies, operas, and excursions. I have learned a great deal of Italian from them, also a lot about Italians. I feel really bad about leaving.

At times I get ambitious and think I'll write an account (one hundred pages at the most) of my impressions of Italy. It could become a book but the exact form of it is still a mystery.

Let's try the thought communication thing which you suggest. See if you can find out the exact time difference between Vancouver and Florence. I am having as much trouble finding this out as I am finding a chart for the Mediterranean heavens in winter. I want to do some star gazing.

I'm glad you got together with my brother and his wife. His comments on the Italians are conventional for people in the military: Italian military men are cowardly, treacherous, etc. I don't think they lack courage when they are fighting for a cause they believe in (e. g. Garibaldi and the fight for independence) or when they are given the right tools to fight with (in North Africa their small tanks, produced by Fiat, were mere peashooters against our larger tanks.) I have also heard that they fought bravely alongside the Germans on the Russian front. It took a lot of courage to man their tiny two man submarines which were able to torpedo a number of our ships in the Mediterranean.

A few days ago I took a trip to Abetone, Florence's nearest skiing mountain. It's in the Apennines maybe forty miles north of here. I left at six a.m. in a lovely subdued sunrise. The bus was full of yelling school kids but across from me were about twelve deaf and dumb people in their late teens. It was marvelous the way they talked with their hands: so swift and expressive. I doubt if they would be allowed to go on a public bus in Canada, but here they are. You also see quite a few blind people in the street here. Maybe Italians don't believe in keeping these unfortunates in an institution. Maybe the government doesn't care much about them. It cost me $3.50 to rent skis and boots at Abetone. A lift pass set me back $3. for the day. This is a real gyp. A Grouse Mountain ski pass goes for only $1.50.

I am enjoying the *Siddharta* which you gave me for Christmas. The style is clear and simple but the ideas are

Florence, Dante and Me

deep. The author is stirring my interest in Buddhism and yoga. Forget the self! Discipline the body! I feel that I am not in very good shape. I have certainly slipped from what I was last year. My weight has gone from 145 to 160. I miss (a bit) the big gym and pool at UBC.

You say that maybe I was born into the wrong nationality. I think you're right. Deep down I wish that I had been born in Italy (but not into a poor family).

March 15, 1961   Florence

Dear J,

I must tell you why I haven't written for eleven days. I really do not like being addressed as "Mr. Pomposity", especially by you, my future wife! I think I admit my faults pretty well. I know I am often too critical of people and things in general but I am not, as you seem to think, "rigorously self-righteous". I am also pretty dogmatic in my tastes in art, music and literature and as I become more knowledgeable, my tastes are becoming even more defined (and refined) and confident. This may seem like arrogance, but I see it as the product of experience and thinking a lot about the paintings I look at, the music I listen to or the books I read. I am starting to realize that my interest in literature, painting, opera, etc. is isolating me more and more from the many people who do not share these interests. I guess it's inevitable and can't be helped. At the same time it's creating a bond with people who share my interests. I try not to look down at people who are 'low brow' but I am not all that successful in this.

And your remark, "We are anything but profound, aren't we?" takes the cake for arrogance (and even contempt!). What's going on? Is there someone new in your life? Sometimes I think you think that I am the one who's comfortably at home among friends and you are the one in Europe living at times a very lonesome existence. And you could have come here if you had had the spirit. And how would you know what depth of thought I reach? I am reading in Italian, thinking in Italian, speaking in Italian. It's a world that's closed to you and you can't judge it. (Although, to be fair, I have to admit that when one studies a new language one must spend a lot of time learning vocabulary, grammar, irregular verbs, etc. and most of this work does not stretch the mind in terms of complexity and abstractions. The time spent on these kinds of things is time that might have been spent on reading challenging books.) I have to admit that you seem to be learning many things, e.g. ethics, Stendahl, naturalism, modern painting, which I haven't much of a clue about. Had I remained at UBC for this year I am sure I would have learnt many things that I have not had time to learn over here.

You find some of my language trite or commonplace. Well, I think maybe you go too far with the notion (inspired by the English Department no doubt!) of "avoiding the expected" (your phrase) in language. ("Oh, my God! How awful! He just used a cliché!") Your principle might apply fairly well to writing, but to speaking? You must admit that we should suit our speech to whomever we are speaking, n'est-ce pas? That university English department of yours (ours!) seems to foster some very artificial ways of expressing oneself. I recall being shot down in red for a bunch of so-called writing errors in freshman year and I still don't see what was wrong with what I wrote! Where do they get their narrow criteria? Why are they so rigid? Don't you, for heaven's sake, be too influenced by them. Such pompous prigs! Ugh!

Also, I don't like pseudo-bohemianism: people who think they're European and cool just because they eat cheese and baguettes and drink wine. We'd do well to have a trial run before getting married. Maybe it will be bliss but maybe bliss broken by terrible fights. I hope not. Sorry, but I have to give you hell the odd time if I am to speak my mind although I dislike causing you any grief when you're so far away.

I'm glad you're enjoying the course on European literature with Woodcock but I can't imagine studying Rimbaud in English. It just doesn't work!

The singing lessons are going very well. La Maestra keeps telling her other pupils what a beautiful voice I have (Ahem!) and how intelligent a pupil I am (Now really!). She is raising my hopes precariously high with remarks like these: "Roberto, you can become a really great popular singer. Bass-baritones of your tonal quality are as rare as virtuous women." Hmmm. I have scrounged some money together and will be buying a guitar so that I can do scales at home.

As I mentioned, we work mostly with parts of scales. It really works! My range is expanding amazingly. I've already increased from a lousy B to a D and eventually hope to absorb the F above that. That's going up. Going down is no problem and I can reach low G with no effort. We don't force anything and I never feel strained or tense. We are expanding my range gradually.

I took a short trip to Pistoia (twenty miles or so north of Florence) by bus the other day. It's got a cathedral and some very narrow medieval streets. The country-side was lovely and green and I saw a group of peasant women dressed in black continuing the ancient practice of washing the family clothes in a stream. Why the black clothes? It might be for mourning, I don't know. Italians often wear a black button or black lapel strip to show that they are grieving. I think this is a good custom and one worth imitating. I watched a bike race but the screaming crowd—hundreds of spectators—was at least as exciting to watch as the cyclists. Rick Bronsdon wasn't in it although he had told me he would be.

I finally got my suit and topcoat. Pure wool and they fit like a glove. The colors are so rich! God, they're lovely!

Rome. The author's Cerruti suit

Castel Sant'Angelo, Rome

I received a friendly letter from Dr. Rotelli, the Italian consul in Vancouver. He was decent enough to reply to the post card I sent him (Several other people didn't).

I got talking with the professor who teaches the history of the Italian language. When I told him that my name was Robert Stuart Thomson he asked me if I was descended from the Stuart kings of England. I had to smile and put him straight.

I read a passage from Verga (who wrote the original *Cavalleria Rusticana* as a short story) the other night and was haunted by the beautiful, wild Sicily that he conjures up. Are you reading him this year? If anyone, Manzoni and Verga should be on that European literature course of yours! 'Bye for now. Must rush off to supper and then to the Pergola theater to see *Tosca*.

[Later that evening] Tosca was a terrible actress but had a sweet Tebaldian voice. The tenor was good on high notes but pot-bellied and couldn't act. Scarpia was powerful and sinister. Having seen Castel Sant'Angelo (in Rome) first hand it certainly helped me to visualize the last act. The audience booed and cat-called and were extremely poor-mannered. The performance wasn't *that* bad!

I have increased my singing lessons to four hours a week.

March 22, 1961

Hello, my Love,

The singing lessons are so much fun. The Maestra was telling me that she had a student once (a bass) who had only one good note, but it was a wonderful note and she could see what it might become. So they worked on exercises for a few years and at the end of that time he had the voice of a real opera singer, a good one, and his range was a couple of octaves. Yesterday I arrived a bit early for a lesson and she was just finishing a lesson with her nephew who is in his mid-twenties, tall and slim, with a goatee. He's a real basso and they were going through the part of Ramfis, the high priest in *Aida*. So powerful is his voice that with certain phrases the whole apartment shook and glasses rattled in the cupboard (my hair just about stood on end, and my eyes bulged out of their sockets!).

Sì, corre voce che l'Etiope ardisca sfidarci ancora,
Yes, the rumor is circulating that the Ethiopian is daring to challenge us again,

E del Nilo la valle, e Tebe minacciar.
And threaten the valley of the Nile and Thebes.

Talk about attentive and exacting! I am allowed to get away with *niente, nothing.* Not one incorrect note. She also has a great imagination (with humor) and will say (We always speak in Italian) things like. "Roberto, sing it again and this time look out the window and pretend that your voice must carry across the Arno to Piazzale Michelangelo!" Or she'll say, "Roberto, fetch that silver plate and we'll use it as a mirror." Then she proceeds to point out something amiss in my breathing or pronunciation. We get along famously. She is such a classic Florentine: articulate, quick-witted, and a bit blunt and satirical. Her language is spiced up with imagery and colorful slang. These lessons are not cheap, but I am really fortunate to have found a teacher of her caliber.

On Saturday I took the train to Siena as part of my "Get to know Tuscany" series. As we headed south to Siena I could see far to the east the fourteen towers of San Gimignano. They look mysterious and beckoning. I haven't visited San Gimignano yet but I will. From the train window I saw three peasants dressed in black walking along, one with flowers, looking like phantoms from another century, characters out of *I Promessi Sposi*. How I'd like to stay and work with a peasant family for a few weeks before coming home! They look so industrious and contented in their work. The Tuscan countryside is incredibly beautiful. I could see a few trees already in blossom and it's getting warm.

On Saturday night I went to a recital of a German soprano at the Chigiana Music Academy, which is apparently famous. Segovia teaches guitar there in the summer. The Siena cathedral is imposing and unusual: gothic with contrasting black and white blocks of marble. I read somewhere that it inspired Wagner's *Parsifal*. There is a library attached to the cathedral and its walls are frescoed by Pinturicchio. What a beautiful way to decorate a library!

Siena as seen from the north-east

Florence, Dante and Me

A little old lady with a shawl on her head showed me Ghiberti's and Donatello's works in the baptistry. When I first looked at her I thought that she might be a *contadina* and that I might have a hard time understanding her dialect. To my surprise, when she opened her mouth to speak her Italian was crystal clear and like something out of a textbook. Maybe it's for good reason that I have heard people say that the Senesi speak the purest Italian. She was so thankful when I gave her a one hundred lira tip. I was glad to give it to her.

Siena: Piazza del Campo and the Torre del Mangia

Sunday I climbed the three hundred fifty foot *Torre del Mangia* (part of the Palazzo Pubblico or town hall) in the center of the city. The tower dwarfs any I have seen in Italy. I went up hundreds of winding, worn, and slippery steps, craning and dodging to avoid knocking my noggin against protruding parts of the staircase, stooping for low passageways, and every once in a while catching sudden and unexpected glimpses of the countryside though small holes in the thick walls. Then, finally, air! Sweet, fresh, and spring-like. What a view! I could see all the medieval city with its winding, narrow streets and, in the distance, the green Chianti hills.

The next morning I went to the main gallery which is very rich in thirteenth and fourteenth century painting and a very strange thing happened. As I looked at Lorenzetti's Madonna I suddenly turned aside and saw the city's roofs through the window. The morning was clear and fresh and as the cathedral bells tolled morning mass and birds chirped at the window ledge I looked at the painting again, heard the wind roar and felt as if it had blown away those six centuries and I was standing there in the thirteenth century, gazing at contemporary art. I had such a feeling of the power of nature in that sudden gust of wind and it tied in so mysteriously with the powerful expression of human faith in the painting and the bells tolling mass that it sent shivers down my spine, I tell you.

Siena was Florence's rival for many years and there were horrendous battles between the two cities. To me they seem poles apart: Florence is lively and business-oriented and has markets and stalls all over the place; Siena is quiet and the streets relatively deserted. Maybe it's got something to do with the railway: Florence is located on the main north-south railroad line, Siena isn't. I find the Senesi friendly and accessible.

I've finished reading *Le Petit Prince*. It's a charming book and its wisdom is presented in such an imaginative way. Thanks for suggesting it.

March 29, 1961   Florence

Hello, you!

I am so glad that we are writing to each other again. Not hearing from you for two weeks was really starting to bug me. But I returned the compliment and you were denied my letters as well. How it hurts me to hurt you! We are both stubborn. Both Taureans. Two bulls! Does that partly account for it? I know you would never have written that "Dear Mr. Pomposity" letter if you had considered how much I need your affection and understanding. Our letters have alternated between flowers and daggers. I love you when you are sweet, gentle, and loving, in short: womanly, and not out to argue all the time.

There are big changes in my life. I have moved. A few weeks ago at the Linguists Club I met an elderly French lady, Méline Méreaux. She›s an artist and her etchings are excellent. I find her very amusing. Her favorite words seem to be "chic" and "aristocrate". She prides herself on knowing a number of Italian nobles (dukes, countesses, etc.) and explains her own non-noble status with the remark: "We French are republican, you know. We didn't have the Revolution for nothing!" (As she says this she looks up at you with big dramatic eyes from her full height of four feet ten.) Her apartment is on the third floor of an old building on the south bank of the Arno, close to the Ponte Vecchio. Mlle.Méreaux knows lots of people so we have lots of visitors for tea or drinks. I am meeting interesting people and speaking a great deal of French. She introduces me as "mon ami italien" so it is never a question of anyone assuming I speak only English and then using me to practice their language skills. Last night we went to a pot-pourri of contemporary French plays on Greek themes.

We have hot water in this apartment. What luxury! (The first time in eight months for me!) Next week we are moving to a large fifth floor apartment in Via Guicciardini, just a block from the Pitti Palace. The building has an old fashioned elevator with a sliding cage-like metal door. Very nineteenth century! There is a terrace with potted plants that looks out onto the Boboli Gardens. I shall practice my guitar and voice there in the morning sun. Right across the street from us is an apartment block with a concrete plaque on it saying *In questa casa visse Nicolò Machiavelli,* etc. (In this house lived Nicolò Machiavelli.)

I took a walk through town the other night (on the north side of the Arno) and stopped for supper in a trattoria. They had two musicians playing: a portly little guy sang lustily and accompanied himself on a mandolin while his friend played guitar. They sang some of my favorites such as *Torna a Sorrento* and *Core Ingrato.* It was a real treat, and so unexpected. A woman in her forties who looked like a streetwalker passed around the collection plate. Many people were singing and dancing and having a good time. I just love it when I happen upon something like this.

Gino arrived back from Naples and we are great buddies again. He had taken some offense at my leaving Ede's.

I don't know why because it had nothing to do with him. I tried to explain things as tactfully as possible. (By the way I hear there's a very good book on tact, a must-read called *International Savoir-Faire.*) Gino has invited me to spend another week with him and his family so next week I will be taking off to Rome and Naples for about two weeks of Easter holidays. I am looking forward to it. There's so much I haven't seen in Rome e. g. the Catacombs, the Baths of Caracalla, the Lateran.

Studying in the Marucelliana Library is wonderful at times, like right now, at dusk, in March, when the buds in the courtyard have burst out and the old palace's courtyard is redolent with their scent. As I sit here in the reading room and gaze up at the many shelves of ancient books I can hear the sad rolling music of an accordeon. It's playing *Parlami d'amore, Mariù./Tutta la mia vita sei tu.* (Speak to me of love, Mariu!/You are my whole life.) I wish you were here to share this with me.

Last Friday I went on a two day excursion to Rimini and San Marino. In Rimini I visited Alberti's Cathedral and the Malatesta Chapel. By late morning it was hot and I went for a swim in the ocean. I was the only one in the water. It was cold, but not that cold, not as cold as the Capilano River in North Vancouver. After the swim I walked along a canal which leads into town. I stopped to chat with some fisherman. In the early afternoon I took the bus to San Marino.

San Marino was cold and very windy but it offered the most breathtaking views I think I have ever seen. The city (which is a republic and independent from Italy) is triangular and sits on the top of a mountain that rises steeply on all sides from the plain below. There are three castles, one on each side of the mountain. One of them is built in such a way that part of it juts out into space: I went inside and took a window seat. When I looked out and *down* there was a straight drop of about one thousand feet. Terrifying! From this window I could see rolling green countryside that seemed to go on forever. In the far distance, eastward, I could make out the blue-green Adriatic and Rimini with her twenty miles of beaches. No one else was in the room and it felt strange to take all of this in alone. There was total silence except for the occasional howling of the wind, the hour-mistaken crowing of a rooster in the valley far below, and the chirping of a few sparrows below the window. You could feel something in the air that said, "Spring is coming!" I splurged on an exotic treat: *torta* (a sweet biscuit kind of cake) with several glasses of Muscatel. They really stung me on the price but I should have asked before ordering. Never assume! I keep having to learn that! I chatted with a couple of female souvenir vendors in their little shop. They asked me, seriously, what part of Italy I was from, even after talking with me for a few minutes. That felt good!

From my new digs here in Florence I can hear a church organ playing as I study. Sonorous music, almost mystical. We had a big supper here last week, a potluck of sorts. I brought Chianti. Guests: an Italian major from Rimini who knew a lot about Italian art, a thirtyish French lady (very tall, who had two terrifying Dobermans whom she called her *"bébés"*) and an elderly woman of fierce aspect and a deep contralto voice but who proved to be a very kind type of person.

The Republic of San Marino as seen from the south-west

In Italy films leave the scene soon after they arrive. I missed *Mai di Domenica* (*Never on Sunday*), which I wanted to see. Halbwachs says it gives a false picture of life in Greece so maybe I didn't miss much. Several of us are going to see the *Scoppio del carro* (explosion of the cart) this Saturday. It takes place on the day before Easter. Four white oxen bedecked in flowers pull a cart full of fireworks through the city and a dove is released and this somehow causes the fireworks to explode. Interesting.

How to be a decadent-looking Italian man: dress elegantly, sport a mustache, and (very important!) wear a large, flashy wristwatch which *must be glanced at noncha-lantly* every now and then.

Women cyclists here are quite noticeable. Some ride around dressed in tight skirts.

Please ask Rachel Giese for the name of that Italian steamship company who hire teachers of English. I sent mother a large bolt of expensive Florentine silk for her to make a dress of. She is good at sewing and appreciates good quality. She'll make something elegant and do it jus-tice. Do you drink that horrible Canadian coffee? Bah! Wait until you try my espresso machine! I am glad you like the shoes I sent you.

April 5, 1961   SanGiuliano,
                                                 just north of Naples

Dearest J,

We (Pat Ballantine, Gino and I) left Florence by train
three days ago. It was a slow over-nighter, leaving at 1:30
a.m. and arriving in Naples at 11:30 a.m. I got into a good
conversation with an American of Calabrese background
who now lives in Italy and works as a truck driver for a soft
drink company. We covered Italian vs. North American
girls (I did most of the listening), the poor job situation in
Canada, and the night school programs in Florence e.g.,
courses offered at The British Institute.

    We received a warm welcome from Gino's family
when we arrived in Torre. I brought a dozen roses for his
mom, which was appreciated. It being Easter the whole
family were dressed in their Sunday best. Nine year old
Maria looked charming in her white dress and white gloves.
For two days we ate our fill, I must say: *Torrese* pasta, salad,
meat and fish (wonderfully fresh) and always enough wine
to get high on. We stayed for two nights and then moved
on to San Giuliano which is on the Volturno River several
miles north of Naples. We spent a day there as guests of
Gino's friend, Antonio.

    San Giuliano is a dusty, sunny little town that still
has a bombed-out look from World War II. (It's quite likely
that my Uncle Ken was here with the New Westminster

Regiment during the war.) You see hundreds of *scugnizzi* (urchins or streetboys) playing in the streets: cute little guys with curly heads and sparkling teeth. They are dusty and dirty but certainly loveable. I could hear shrill cries echoing from a nearby courtyard where about twenty of these little rascals were playing leap-frog. All this energy! Everyone seems to have it. Maybe it's in the very soil and they get it from Vesuvius. Neapolitans I find friendly, spontaneous and very musical. A characteristic expression which I hear a lot is *roba bona* (nice stuff). It can be used to describe pasta, wine and nice-looking girls. *Per me tu sei roba bona.* (For me you're the cat's meow.)

Antonio is a short, powerfully built character. He showered us with southern warmth and hospitality: pasta, fish, meat, vino, and with the usual promptings of *Mangia! Mangia! Non ti preoccupare!* (Eat! Don't worry!) In spite of the tragic events in his life Antonio seems such a cheerful person. Both his parents died when he was only seven and the only sign of them is two stiff, dark, somber portraits which command the whole room. Ten out of twelve of Antonio's children died either at birth or at a very young age. Who knows of what? Their 'house' is one large room dominated by a huge bed in which two cute little girls were pretending to sleep (when they weren't looking at us— Strange Canadians!—and giggling and chatting away.) We listened to some Caruso on Antonio's record player and I was amazed by the clarity of the sound. I had never really heard Caruso until then. What a voice! It's strange that he did not sound this good on the expensive stereo sytems back in Canada.

One day, after returning to Gino's, we went on a long drive down the Almalfi coast. Gino's mom packed a large basket of boiled eggs, baloney, bread. cake, wine and our bathing suits. We left at five a.m., driving off into the morning haze and grey-white light. The road leading south hugs the coast. It is hilly and winds all over the place. The panoramas are amazing! We pass right by the place where Circe tried to lure Ulysses to his destruction on the rocks. Almost everywhere you look there are terraced vineyards and orchards, many of lemon trees. Italians sure know how to make the most of their mountainous land. In this season the lemons are huge. We stopped at the side of the road to ask directions of a small boy. He doesn't pay the slightest heed to our question and thrusts two fistfuls of lemons in our faces: *Volete limoni?* (Do you want lemons?) he asks with that persistent, whining, wheedling tone that the Neapolitan dialect can convey so well. Our response to his action was spontaneous: we all laughed like hyenas and carried on our way.

We stopped at the Emerald Grotto (discovered in 1932): wondrous shades of blue, fantastic stalagmites and the most eerie, unusual effects of sound and filtered light.

On the way back we veered off from the main road and followed a side road down to a little cove, complete with a Saracen tower on the cliffs surrounding it. Imagine the Saracens being here! When? Maybe the ninth century? I imagine there is lots of Moorish blood in the people who live in the south. Italians often refer to Southern Italy as "il Mezzogiorno" which literally means noon i.e. hot. About a month ago at Ede's Magda referred to Naples as *"laggiù nell'Africa"* (down there in Africa) in the presence of Gino. I think she did it to get a rise out of him. She sure did. He glared at her and remonstrated with the classic *"Ma che laggiù nell'Africa!"* (said with the furrowed brow). He took similar umbrage with me one evening when he visited my room and noticed the huge (about four feet square) map of Italy that I have on the wall. It's extremely detailed and even shows elevations. I find it useful for studying the country.

Photo of the Amalfi coast looking north

The trouble is: it was pricey and I didn't feel I could afford the bottom half of the map (from Rome south). Gino was very annoyed that the bottom half was missing. Did I think that it was less important than the top half? I tried to explain but I still got the furrowed brow treatment and a look of disgust. He didn't seem convinced.

Florence, Dante and Me

Anyway, back to my story! In the little cove with the Saracen tower I went for a swim. I was the only one who went in. For some reason the water seemed saltier than I expected but it was refreshing, blue-green and crystal-clear. I was luxuriating in it and when I stretched out my hand it touched something large. I recoiled quickly and let out a roar. It turned out to be a large dead dog. *Che schifo!* (How disgusting!) Who knows how the poor creature ended up in the ocean?

April 13, 1961   Florence

Ciao, Bella!

I just got back to Florence yesterday and got your letter.
There's a lot to tell you about.

I am back to my voice lessons and they are going
well. At 20,000 lire a month (out of my 60,000 lire stipend)
you can imagine if it hurts! But my voice has acquired so
much power and range that sometimes I am actually dumb-
founded by my sounds and break off in wonder half way
through a passage. Maestra Del Vivo is pleased, of course.
She's so conscientious and honest! We plan to make a tape
recording of one of our lessons. It will help me to keep on
track as I continue practicing back in Canada. Maestra Del
Vivo is very proud of her other favorite pupil, her nephew
Rinaldo, who did so well in a competition in Milan last week.
She's an amusing lady. I almost burst myself laughing at her
when she mimics my mistakes, singing through her nose,
singing cross-eyed or singing out the side of the mouth. I
soon smarten up. She has huge, expressive eyes and a quick
mind. In my opinion she combines three common Florentine traits: dignity, style and buffoonery. She has agreed to
let me try a few songs so I am working on *My Funny Val-
entine* and the theme from *High Noon*: *Do not forsake me, oh
my darlin'*. Both are well suited to my voice.

To catch you up on the last week or so: We (Pat and I)
left Gino's with a warm farewell. We took the *Circumvesuviana*

train into Naples where Pat and I spent the day. I like Naples and find that it's growing on me. The downtown looks very baroque and has a faded elegance which gives it charm. Before long we decided we had to have a pizza. After all, Naples is the place where the stuff was invented. As we sat there eating our pizzas we were serenaded by a strolling mandolin player. He played mostly classic Neapolitan songs like *Dicitencello Vuje* . I have always associated the mandolin with Naples so for me it was the perfect touch.

In the late afternoon we went down to the water-front by the Norman Castel del Ovo where I rented a rowboat. We rowed out to sea and then turned north-wards, past the fish traps of Santa Lucia and, further on, to the wind-ravaged remains of an old castle. It was beau-tiful to pause and just let ourselves be rocked by the waves and look back at the ancient city with its volcano. Then we watched the sun set over Capri and the Bay. For me Napoli is above all else the city of Caruso and if time per-mits I am going to seek his house out. It's probably in the slums and I am hoping that that area was not bombed flat in World War II. In the evening we went to see *Madame Butterfly* at the San Carlo Opera House. I think it dates from the mid-1700s. It's certainly baroque: sumptuous and ornate. Inside you sit down and look around and you are transported in a flash back to the days of Verdi. The performance was not great (weak tenor) but it was a thrill to be at San Carlo.

The second day in Naples we took the boat to Capri. The sea on this crossing is a dark bottle-green. I have never seen a color like it in nature. The blue grotto was also a marvel. I felt the water and it is very cold. From the town of Capri we took a bus to Anacapri, the peak of which is about one thousand feet above sea level. You can stand on the spot where one of the craziest Roman emperors (Tiberius, I think) used to sit and amuse himself by watching his attendants throw slaves off the high cliff. Nice guy! From this cliff top I could see the ocean spread out before me like a plate of light blue glass. To my right I could see Sorrento and the Amalfi Coast. The silence was broken only by the rustling of leaves. *Vedi Napoli poi muori.* [33]

The following day Pat stayed in Naples to visit a family friend and I took the train to Rome. I contacted Jaqub, my Jordanian friend from Perugia last summer. He was so kind about showing me how to get adjusted to the city. He is now studying medicine at the University of Rome. Imagine! Studying medicine not in Arabic, but in Italian! I admire his courage. Jaqub gave me the address of a room where some of his friends used to stay. It was very cheap so I thought it would be a good idea. Big mistake! It turned out to be a small room with half a dozen people sleeping there: snoring, sniffing and probably sick! I tried sleeping for a few hours and then left and went to an all-night bar where I spent the rest of the night reading. Never again!

I don't know what possessed me but the following day I decided to get shaved by a barber. This was a first for me! What luxury! And only 340 Lire (about fifty cents). In the afternoon I visited the church of *San Pietro in Vincoli* (Saint Peter in Chains) to see the statue of Moses by Michelangelo. It really conveys the spiritual power of

Moses, at least as I see him. In the evening I went to the Teatro Argentina to see *The Tales of Hoffman*. It wasn't great but I didn't know the music beforehand so I couldn't do it justice. This is the opera house where the premiere of Rossini's *Barbiere di Siviglia* was sabotaged by a hostile pro-Paisiello group who were paid to boo and hiss. I left early and walked through Rome in the night. It's spring and the blossom-perfumed air was elating.

Bust of Caracalla

On the way back to Florence (near Assisi) I extended my hand to help a little old man hop up onto the moving train. Disgusted with his lack of vigor in old age, he muttered bitterly in real Roman style "*Managgia, la vecchiaia!*" (Translated loosely: "Son of a bitch, old age!")

Gino has fallen in love with Pat. Now there's two opposites, those two! It will be interesting to see where that goes. She is so quiet and modest. He is high energy, emotion, and flair! I am glad you like the postcard of Caracalla. I didn't see the original but I found this postcard so arresting (what with that piercing stare of his) that I couldn't resist sending it to you.

Some Italian salesmen are really persistent. One tried to tell me that the 1.15 meter belt that I was looking at would fit me (with a 34 inch waist!).

April 20, 1961   Florence

Dearest J,

It's a rainy Sunday afternoon and I am alone in my quiet
room, with only the gentle patter of rain on the roof tiles
and the faint whining of scooters in the street below. Florence after an April shower is special. I look out onto the
Boboli Gardens, so rich and green, and hear the birds give
forth an exultant chorus. The pines smell fresh and the sky
really is a robin's egg blue. The clouds are mushrooming
up, amassed by the huffing breath of a giant who ascends
the Arno from the sea. Hey, you say you are showing my
letters to all kinds of people on campus, including professors. Do tell: *which professors?* I am all ears! What is their
reaction? Do you think these letters could ever become
part of a book? *A Canadian Student in Italy?*

The Boboli Gardens

The other day I took a train down the river to Pisa and heard Professor Luigi Russo talk on literature. According to Rachel Giese at UBC he's one of the most famous literary critics in Italy. He looks typically Sicilian (sez me who have never been to Sicily!): a large, Buddha-type head and enormous dark eyes that gleam when he's inspired. One of his ideas that stuck with me is that we should look for what is good in a work of art. It doesn't sound that deep but it's good common sense: so many critics seem to be obsessed with looking for flaws and shortcomings and showing how clever they are. And then I got to thinking: "Yes, and maybe we should look for the good in a nation, and in individuals." Being myself of a very critical bent I find this hard to do. I realize this is a shortcoming and something I have to work on.

A few days ago I went to see Fellini's *La Strada* (with Anthony Quinn) at the Film Society. It's pretty brutal and violent in parts but it shows an interesting group of characters who tour the Italian countryside putting on a small circus (tight-rope walking, a strong man act, etc.) I preferred it to *La Dolce Vita* which has much to do with aimlessness. After the movie some professor made a few points and then tried to get some discussion rolling. It could be me but I did not enjoy the discussion. A lot of subtlety and maybe originality but not much of substance. Maybe the Italian language is partly to blame. It sounds so gorgeous and eloquent and it has so many rhetorical flourishes. It must be easy to get carried away. Here are Turiddu's lines to Santuzza in *Cavalleria Rusticana*. Notice the power achieved by putting three adjectives in row before the noun: "*questa vana tua gelosia*".

Bada, Santuzza, schiavo non sono di questa vana tua gelosia!

Watch out, Santuzza, I am not a slave to this useless jealousy of yours!

This makes for a very powerful line, especially with the music that goes with it.

I am still not sure about the summer. I would like to spend it in France if possible because it will be four or five years at least before I get over here again. I plan to finish the B.A. then do an M.A. and Ph.D., to be followed by a few years of teaching.

What a mess our world is in! Mlle Méreaux is very worried about the Algerian situation. The treacherous behavior of General Challe! *"Il est abominable!"* says she.

April 30, 1961   Florence

Dearest J,

It's a cloudy, rainy Sunday afternoon here but it's a very special day for me. I am now twenty-one. I have come of age and I am not the only one either, am I!? You beat me to it by three days. Many happy returns, Love! I hope you did something very special for your birthday. And thanks for the telegram—such a pleasant surprise! I will drink a toast to our happiness and autonomy!

I went to mass this morning with Mlle Méreaux at the church of the *Badia Dantesca* where we heard Florence's mayor, La Pira, give a sermon on the lives of the saints. This wonderful man distributes bread and money to the poor every Sunday at the church. He's a legend around the city. Mlle Méreaux introduced me to him, which was a thrill. She also insisted on treating me to a steak lunch, which was a nice gesture to help me celebrate my birthday.

I'm glad you had a chance to talk with my mother. She is great at times when it comes to hitting the nail on the head. She also has a lot of common sense and intuition. It's too bad she doesn't read at all! (So important for developing the mind). Dante might have put her with the *accidiosi,* the slothful, in Purgatory. I am glad the course on modern art is going well. I know very little about it and look forward to some lectures from you.

The tall spire is part of the Badia Dantesca

I have been watching Italian parents with their children and I'm not sure what to think. Do they tend to spoil them? They certainly dress them beautifully and show them all kinds of attention. They are obviously proud of them and I don't think I've seen one kid misbehave in public. I strongly suspect that they have happier childhoods than Canadian children and I think they grow into adults who are confident and generally outgoing. This is a good thing although at times self-confidence goes too far and becomes cockiness, intolerance and self-centeredness—not good things! Still, I guess it's better to mollycoddle kids rather than ignore them or squelch them. There is nothing worse than thinking you're not worth much and ending up shy and lacking in self-confidence.

I'm still in the COTC. [Canadian Officers Training Corps]. If we have a full depression I can always put in a summer at Camp Shilo [in Manitoba] and make some money. I would also get my officer's commission in the Reserve. Isn't Gagarin's space flight amazing? Where will it lead?

In a coffee bar the other day I was reading about Eichmann. I damn near puked at some of the atrocities committed by those damned Nazis. One Jewish man who tries to escape from a mass burial pit is clubbed to death for his trouble. Another is torn to pieces by an S.S. officer's dog. Eichmann just stood by and watched people being clubbed to death or torn apart by dogs. What a monster! I am reading about such things as these in the newspapers here; I don't recall ever reading similar things in our Canadian newspapers.

Have you ever studied to organ music? I can hear one right now in a nearby church.

Mlle Méreaux and I have a great time gabbing away in French, Italian, and sometimes English.

I have always liked Baudelaire but recently I have been reading some new poems by him and have to say that I have fallen under his spell. Let me give you a taste. In a poem called *Les Phares* (The Lighthouses) he describes the essence of those great painters who have left a truly noble legacy to mankind. In just a few short lines he captures their essence. Here is what he writes about Leonardo da Vinci:

> Léonard de Vinci, miroir profond et sombre,
> *Leonardo da Vinci, deep and somber mirror*
>
> Où des anges charmants, avec un doux souris
> *Where charming angels, with a sweet smile*

Tout chargé de mystère, apparaissent à l'ombre
Pregnant with mystery appear in the shadow

Des glaciers et des pins qui ferment leur pays,
Of the glaciers and pins which enclose their country.

I was in ecstasy the other day at Maestra Del Vivo's. She played an LP of Sinatra's *Only the Lonely* for me. We both love the richness of his voice and the sensitivity of his interpretations.

I miss my Sinatra records. He was a major source of controversy in my family: my mother loves "Frankie" (which is the name she goes by as well); my stepfather finds him sleazy and much prefers Bing Crosby, whom he finds more manly and wholesome. My stepfather is thirteen years older than my mother; maybe that has something to do with it.

I haven't seen Gino since he has gone nuts over Patricia. I am feeling a bit resentful. Maybe I shouldn't feel this way but I do.

I am not going to galleries as much as I did a few months ago; I am too busy getting ready for the exams coming up.

May 7, 1961   Florence, 11 Via Guicciardini

My dear J,

I spoke to my Italian professor about the exams in June. He said I would be tested on ten cantos from *The Divine Comedy.* I also will be tested on the major works of Ugo Foscolo (very complex—an early romantic, supersensitive and maybe a bit suicidal.) I guess you could say he's the Italian Keats (as far as that goes). The exam will include written and oral exams in French. My friend, Dr. Halbwachs, has kindly offered his help to case the oral together. He'll be one of the profs interrogating me on June 6, my D day. I hope to get at least half a year's credit (nine units) from UBC. We'll see. I should get it but the systems are so different that I am not overly optimistic. I'm really going to have to hit the books. It's too bad in a way because I shall have to decline Rick Bronsdon's invitation to spend a week at his place up in the mountains.

Lectures end on May 20th. Exams are open to one's choice: June 6 or June 21. They comprise oral and written parts.

At times I think I'm too influenced by literature although isn't rewarding when the new experiences we acquire serve to illuminate those experiences we read of in books? (Or, to look at it another way, when what we read in books reflects what we have experienced ourselves.) I find that I understand (or maybe *feel*) Dante's Ulysses (canto 25) much better now that I have been roaming around Italy, separated from my lady love just as he had to wander around the Mediterranean before being united with Penelope.

Né il debito amore
Neither the due (promised) love

Lo qual dovea Penelope far lieta
Which should have made Penelope happy

Vincer poter dentro di me l'ardore
Overcome within me the ardor
(Could overcome the ardor within me)

Ch'io ebbi a divenir del mondo esperto
that I had to become experienced in the world

E dei vizi umani e del valore.
Both its vices and virtues.

How well Dante expresses it! He sees value even in exploring evil, the dark side of human behavior. I really like that in him. He had a brave spirit and an inquisitive mind. I am learning a lot in the way of practical revelations like this from my year in Italy. It has been a great experience!

Please price Peppino di Capri records for me. I'll pick up some here if they can't be found in Vancouver. I'm really big on his style! Lyrical and passionate. Great to dance to. What's happening? Your last letter sounded like a dutiful business letter. Thanks so much for the nice birthday gift—an encyclopedia of the opera! I will treasure it.

May 12, 1961   Florence

Dearest J,

I am very happy to get your letter. A knock at my door this morning. A little Chihuahua face sticks her head in: Mlle. Méreaux. *J'ai quelque chose de très bon pour toi, qui commence avec un «l»!* By this time I'm barking and jumping around! And such a nice, newsy letter it was!

Mlle M. has a few manias: she eats lots of lemons, shuts doors so quietly that you can't hear them close, and she eats absolutely everything on her plate (a habit from World War Two). She gets up every day at five a.m.! She's a big help and corrects (tactfully) my spoken French and suggests improvements on my essays. It's almost as if I were living in France which is great because my French is too bookish. Funny, I didn't need to go to Laval to improve my spoken French after all; I am improving it here.

May is as hot as blazes here and studying is impossible at times. I saw Queen Elizabeth the other day in the Piazza della Signoria. She was on a throne about ten yards from me. It was quite a sight: all kinds of people in medieval costume including trumpeters who blazed forth fanfares. I was transported back in time to the 1300s!

As usual I am running out of money and the Italian government informs me that the scholarship is not renewable and ends on June 30. So I will be returning to Vancouver in late June! I can't wait to see you! It's been such a long time!

Mlle Méreaux often has people in for afternoon tea. Sometimes countesses! She introduces me as *"mon fils spirituel"*, which is amusing. *"Spirituel"* can mean both spiritual and witty. I go through the ritual and bow slightly, *Molto piacere, Contessa!* Another visitor is an actor who performs in Goldoni's plays. He looks like he stepped right out of the eighteenth century: fine features, aquiline nose and all. I can certainly imagine him in a powdered wig.

We had other visitors too: a tall guy named "Berry" from Belgium and his sister, at least I assumed it was his sister and referred to her as such until Berry himself put me straight—she was his *amante*. Naive, provincial me! I had to laugh at this. Anyway, we all got along well and they have invited me to stay at their place in Brussels. I would but I won't have time. Rats! This is not the first time I have been invited by Europeans to visit them in their home. I get the impression that Europeans are much more generous than Canadians when it comes to offering hospitality and friendship.

Thanks for sending information on the summer courses. Is the Bible course given by the English department any good? I'd find a course in Bible literature invaluable. It would certainly help me to understand most of the great art, sculpture, etc. that I have been studying this past year! I can't believe how pagan my upbringing and education have been!

I expect UBC will give me six credits (out of 18) towards an honors B.A. for my year over here but nothing is certain and we shall see.

I am glad I moved to Via Guicciardini. This part of town is much brighter and sunnier than the gloomy, narrow streets of Ede's neighborhood although I have to admit that I miss that gang! I have broken a good attachment and probably offended them and I don't feel good about it. Still, I think overall I have made a good choice. My new apartment is quite large and newly decorated. Mlle Méreaux is intellectually stimulating. We speak mostly French so I am learning a lot of everyday French from her. Even talking about the weather is good practice. At the moment my French is improving and my Italian slipping a little. *Strano ma vero.*

I am half way through Dante's *Paradiso*. It's loaded with medieval theological doctrine and very difficult, more difficult than the *Inferno* or *Il Purgatorio*. I am cramming for the exams which are coming up in about three weeks. I will take three: Italian-French translation (written), Italian literature (oral) and French literature (oral). Just imagine: Professor Walter Binni, one of the best literary critics in the country, will be there! Yikes!

I had another letter from R. today giving me the address of a shipping company which hires crew for the Atlantic crossing. A job like this would be a big help financially. It would save me $200.

May 28, 1961   Florence, 11 Via Guicciardini

Dear J.

I am quite peeved not to have heard from you for two
weeks. Maybe I should spend the summer in France and
not come home until September. Thanks for looking into
summer jobs for me. There seems to be ziltch! It's not
going to be easy to think about scrounging money up, etc.
again after this lovely (and dearer as time goes by) year's
sojourn in Italy. Not only this, but I'm going to miss lots
here: the food, the history and great art all around me.
I'll even miss the dusty streets! It is decidedly with mixed
emotions that I think of my return to Vancouver. I wonder
how we're going to find each other.

The past few weeks I have been absorbed in books.
I have done all I am going to do (re. the exam) on Dante
and Foscolo. I still should read some literary critics (Binni,
Croce, etc.) and Rousseau's *Confessions* but doubt I'll have
time. I have just learned that *Oberman* is not on the exam.
Now they tell us! Actually, it doesn't matter because I never
did read it; in fact, I was never able to find it. None of
the bookstores stocked it so I guess no one in charge ever
ordered it. *Molto strano.*

I am planning on leaving for France on June seventh.
After June second please send any mail to me c/o American
Express, 9 rue Scribe, Paris IVième). I am thinking of doing
two summer courses in French literature this summer. One

is on the seventeenth century (Professor Daniel Poirion of Yale), the other is on twentieth century literature (Professor Jean Darbelnet of Laval). Both men have outstanding reputations. I am looking forward to this. **[34]**

There was a magnificent rainbow this evening. It stretched in a perfect arc from Fiesole to the mists over Belvedere. There was a fine spray in the warm May air and the city's towers and palaces were lit in gold.

I saw *Turcaret* by LeSage at La Pergola Theater the other night. It's a good satire on a nouveau riche character. It was directed by Jean Vilar himself and there was even music by Duke Ellington. As you know, Vilar is one of my idols. In freshman year at UBC I bought an LP of him reciting a selection of great French poetry. I listened to it dozens of times, reciting the poems with him and trying to imitate his sounds and cadences. This process helped me to acquire a good accent. Get this: my mother told me months later that she wondered if I had had a French priest in my bedroom! For tonight I've a ticket for *Lohengrin* (in German) at the Teatro Communale, which has just reopened. I am looking forward to my first Wagner.

I was having supper this evening when a blind man came in and sat down across from me. He looked very ill at ease. I said some friendly words to him and noticed how grateful he was to be spoken to with kindness. With a little imagination I put myself in his place, *felt* and not *saw* which was knife and which was fork, and so on, and was almost moved to tears. How sad it is to be blind! Why are there so many blind people here? Or maybe it just seems that way because they are visible in the street and don't seem

Florence, Dante and Me

to be confined in institutions. It's a rough, fast-moving and crowded society.

I have tentative plans to leave France for Canada by boat around June 20. I could fly but I really enjoy crossing the Atlantic by ship. In Paris on the way home I plan to buy several books (e. g. a good dictionary). I hear that the prices are very cheap.

Please ask my brother for information about the Ontario automobile company which hires people to drive their cars out to British Columbia. Maybe I could be a driver.

June 13, 1961   Paris

Dear J,

I arrived here by train via Milan and picked up your letter
at the American Express. How useful these people at the
American Express are! And how beautiful it is along the
Seine in the afternoon sun, watching river boats chugging
along. I saw *Hiroshima Mon Amour* at the movies last night.
A real work of art! As arranged, I have met up with Dave
Trott who is in France for the summer on a two month
scholarship paid for by the Lafarge Cement Company. The
purpose of the scholarship is to give a real taste of life
in France to some outstanding student of French at the
university. Everything is paid for, travel and all expenses.
Dave will travel all over France and will be hosted by many
people. What a great way for him to learn real conversational French! Some scholarship! **[35]**

In a few days Dave will be touring the Loire Valley
and he has kindly arranged three days of accommodation
for me. In the meantime I'm staying at a very cheap hotel
near the Sorbonne: Monsieur le Prince. I am struck by
the similarity between Quebec City and Paris. It's the
architecture, a seventeenth century kind of look. This
afternoon we walked around the city, admiring Notre
Dame's towers, etc.

I haven't told you about my emotional leave-taking in
Florence last week. I managed to visit most of my friends.

I was really choked up when Maestra Del Vivo looked fondly at me and said, *"Bob, ti ho visto tanto volentieri!"* (It's hard to translate this but paraphrased it means more or less "It's been a great pleasure to meet with you.") I'll never forget the tingling down my spine as I descended her apartment steps for the last time in who knows how many years, maybe never. Maestra Del Vivo embodies everything I admire in Florentines: high standards of artistry, intelligence, and good-natured buffoonery. Then I rode my bike over to the west side of town and sold it back to Signor Sgherzi.

Back in Vancouver: Myself, Dave Trott and his sister Jo

This was followed by a visit to Ede Parenti's place and a parting glass of Cognac. Gino was in Naples so I didn't get to see him. I still feel a bit bad about leaving Ede's place. She showed me a lot of kindness but it had become far too noisy. We parted good friends. That night I had my last supper at Italia's trattoria and received a warm "buon viaggio" from her, her husband and her son, Filippo. All these Florentines have enriched my life with their beautiful language, their ideas, and, above all, their friendship. **[36]**

I passed the exams (21 out of 30 in French; 19 out of 30 in Italian). I am not used to such low marks but given the circumstances they are probably not that bad. This is a university for Italians and I am only a *straniero*. I was lucky I was able to talk them into letting me take the exams; no one else was allowed to because the professors had gone on strike a few days earlier and had shut the place down. I told them that if I didn't take the exams I wouldn't get any credit from UBC. I also heard good news from UBC. They are giving me 12 units (out of a possible 18) for my work in Italy. This means if I do two upper division French courses this summer I will be back on track for finishing my honors B.A. one year from now. I shall have to leave La Belle France around June 23 and get back to Vancouver. I will sign off now. This might be my last letter from Europe. I can't wait to see you!

Last Sunday Dave Trott and I and a couple of French ladies (friends!) went for a country drive. We visited Fontainebleau then stopped in a charming rural hamlet nearby, Moret-sur-Loing, for a three hour long lunch. French style! We walked along the river banks and looked at the artwork. Beautiful country: weeping willows, poplars, old river mills, and miniature castle residences. You could just imagine Monet standing outdoors at his easel. *Je suis amoureux de la France!* We went to the apartment of one of the girls and listened to records (and sang) until about midnight, then Dave and I walked for miles, all the way to the Arc de Triomphe and back.

A few days ago I looked up our friend R and went with her to the Louvre. I didn't need too much in the way of a guide because I recognized instantly many of the artists I had studied in Florence. How satisfying it was to be able to do that! Yesterday I went to the Jeu de Paume art gallery to see *les impressionistes*. Of all the artists there I prefer Gauguin, especially his native women. I plan to go back tomorrow. What a choice of cultural activity there is in this city! I wish I had more time! Last night I went with Dave to see Helen Hayes in *The Glass Menagerie*. A great actress in an excellent play. After a few drinks we went for the longest of walks: the whole Champs-Elysées and then some! Tomorrow night it's Racine's *Andromaque* at the Comédie Française. This morning I saw the house where Baudelaire was born. He is high on my list of great poets. The Rodin museum really impressed me, especially his statue of Paolo and Francesca kissing. (Dante seems to pop up everywhere.) I think Rodin's best work is on the same level as Michelangelo's. In the late afternoon we climbed the tower of Notre Dame. The gargoyles from the roof are an amazing sight. On June fifteenth Dave and I are off to Tours for a three day tour of the Loire Valley and its castles. *La gloire de la France ancienne!* Then I leave for Canada from Le Havre on June 20th.

Salve, Musa!

Here we are in the beautiful valley of the Loire, 230 km. south-west of Paris. This wide grey-brown river meanders its way through a fertile plain: green fields, yellow alders, and straight regal-looking lines of Lombardy poplars. Dave and I rented Vespas today. The first time for both of us. We had quite a laugh when he started his up, floored it, and roared up onto the sidewalk. I thought for sure that he was going to fly it through the front door of the rental shop!

At the badly damaged castle of Cinq Mars we had a guide, a friendly little Frenchwoman who trilled her r's and thought it was a hoot that we took her for the owner of the castle. One of the towers she showed us had been a German observation post in World War II. I noticed the name "Scüdler" (doubtless a German soldier) carved on the scaffolding; it fitted in well with the swords, halberts and crossbows we had seen inside the castle and it set me brooding on the tragedy of war and how it always manages to raise its ugly head. I thought of my stepfather who was gassed (and permanently damaged) in World War One and of my Uncle Ken who had slogged over dozens of Italian mountains fighting the Germans in World War II.

We visited two other castles (Langlais, Villandry). Both are impressive. Then we had a nice surprise in the evening. An official from the Alliance Française came by in his huge car and took us out to supper at Villandry. Wow! Did he roar over those country roads! I was in the back seat but I saw the speedometer: 130 km. per hour! After supper (and much, much wine) we went to an outdoor *son et lumière* concert given in the courtyard of one of the castles. [37] Performing was the Montjoie choir from Paris. The music was a good blend of religious and folk and sitting there enjoying it all I found myself thinking of France's two great Renaissance poets: Ronsard and DuBellay. In the background we could see a blazing red sphere of a sun dropping slowly over the Loire.

During the intermission we were introduced to a few local notables: the mayor, his wife, and the prefect. The mayor asked us how old we were: "Twenty-one" we answered. Hearing this, he quipped self-pleasedly: "*Tous ceux qui aiment ont vingt ans.*" (All those who love are twenty.) I made a good impression, I think, by saying that I found the evening's performance even better than those I had seen at the Pitti Palace in Florence. (Maybe not true, but it was diplomatic!) After the concert they put on unannounced readings by actors in period costumes at various places on the castle grounds. We were walking in the maze of high hedges in the Italian garden when we suddenly heard loud voices coming out of the hedges somewhere. We listened carefully. They seemed to be coming from the other side of a hedge, a man and a woman talking. When we looked behind the hedge, sure enough, there was a couple dressed in Renaissance costumes. It was a thrill to recognize the poem that they were acting out. It was by Ronsard and it's about a young suitor, Ronsard himself, who warns his lady love that if she spurns him she will bitterly regret it when she is old and he has become a famous poet:

> Je serai sous la terre et fantôme sans os,
> Par les ombres myrteux je prendrai mon repos.
> Vous serez au foyer une vieille accroupie
>
> Regrettant mon amour et votre fier dédain.
> Vivez, si m'en croyez, n'attendez à demain:
> Cueillez dès aujourd'hui les roses de la vie.

> *I will be in the earth and, boneless phantom,*
> *Near myrtle shadows I will take my rest.*
> *You will be at the hearth a hunched-over old woman*
>
> *Regretting my love and your proud scorn.*
> *Live, if you believe me, don't wait for tomorrow:*
> *Pick the roses of life starting from today.*

Seeing that Dave and I both appreciated Ronsard our host drove us out to the cemetery, right then and there, to visit the poet's grave. The cemetery at midnight was enchanting: dark and perfectly still, the only sound being the occasional croak of a frog. Then the three of us went for a tasty meal of rabbit and boiled rice *à la calabrese* washed down with several bottles of wine. We were all feeling the wine and chatted and joked away for two hours. Then we went for drinks to his place. Out on the balcony of his fifth floor apartment he made a flamboyant gesture embracing the whole town and called it his "petit Chicago". *Intéressant.* I wonder what he meant exactly.

The castle of Chenonceaux

Today Dave and I took in three more castles: Amboise, Chaumont, and Chenonceaux. Chenonceaux is extraordinary because it juts right out onto the river. Tomorrow I leave for Paris, thence to Le Havre to board my ship: Greek Line, the *Arkadia*, 23,000 tons, two swimming pools. I hope it's good! It will make a short stop in Cork, Ireland but I don't know if we can go ashore. I am arriving in Montreal on June 28th and will be flying CPA to Vancouver (only $110.) that same night. I'm coming home! It will be so great to see you! It's been a long, long time!

END

Footnotes

1   (p. 3) I am referring to the old campus of Laval, which was in the *haute ville*. In 1960 the university was just beginning to expand westwards to Sainte Foy. Maurice Duplessis had been the premier of the province for many years and had stubbornly refused to accept any financial aid from the federal government. He hurt no one but himself and the people of Quebec.

2   (p. 3) I didn't realize at the time that this friendly, modest man who was also interested in Baudelaire was none other than *the* Gilles Vigneault who was destined to become one of  the most popular French-Canadian singers of all time. His *Mon Pays, c'est L'hiver* from the 1960s is his best known song.

3   (p. 8) As the year progressed I became familiar with the portraits of such great painters as Leonardo da Vinci, Bronzino, Perugino and Raphael. Their subjects are proud and richly dressed and so too are many of the modern Italians whom I observed while taking

the *passeggiata* in the Corso Vannucci. Pride, flair, taste—I think these are bred to the bone in Italians.

4 (p. 18) Looking back years later (2016) I think it was neither wise nor necessary to make "Italian only, no English" a rigid policy. It would have been better to strike a balance and cultivate both Italian and English-speaking friends throughout the year. My stubborn "rule" caused me to suffer unnecessarily at times from loneliness and isolation.

5 (p. 24) *La Festa della Rificolona* (September 7) celebrates the birth of the Virgin Mary (supposedly in Nazareth) on a September 8. On this date many Florentines mill about town carrying lanterns and singing as they make their way down to the celebrations on the Arno.

6 (p. 33) This German artillery tactic is described with droll dark humor by the Canadian author Farley Mowat in his World War II memoir, *And No Birds Sang* (Vancouver: Douglas and McIntyre, reprint of 2012. See pages 84-87.) The scene: Sicily. Mowat is sitting on a bren gun carrier and is part of a Canadian force advancing on a German-held hill town. All is calm and nature-loving Mowat is bird watching with his binoculars. All of a sudden: Pandemonium! Well aimed German artillery suddenly comes crashing down all over the place. Mowat and another soldier bolt to a ditch at the side of the road. As the bombardment continues Mowat yells out to his companion the names of the German guns as he is able to identify them: "81 mm. medium mortars...MG-42s... four-barrelled Flakvierling light anti-aircraft mount", etc.

Regarding Alfredo (at the Bianchi *pensione* in Perugia) I should mention that one evening we had a very strenuous wrestling match in the living room. I forget how it started. He got the better of me eventually but I think I gave him a run for his money.

7   (p. 37) Len Timbers was a friend who owned a record shop on Robson Street. He specialized in classical music and had an amazing knowledge of the field. I mention him in the introduction as well.

8   (p. 39) Prices to enter galleries, museums, etc. were very low in 1960. I was fortunate. One paid nothing to wander around the Forum or the Baths of Caracalla. Today it costs you about $20 to visit either. To tour the Vatican now (2016) will set you back $25. In those days it cost about a dollar. Back in 1960 there was no need to make reservations and pay in advance for visits. In 2016 it is necessary to make a reservation if you want to avoid huge line ups. Another big change I've noticed concerns graffiti. There were hardly any in 1960. Alas! that's no longer the case.

9   (p. 45) Dr. Leonard Grant. (1912-ca.1963) I started university with no Latin but as a student in honors Romance languages (French and Italian) I was wisely advised to take at least one year of both Latin and German. Any good graduate school would demand a reasonable knowledge of them. Dr. Grant was a mine of interesting lore on the civilization of ancient Rome and this made his classes fascinating. He was also the most organized, clear lecturer I ever encountered. At the beginning of every class he would take five minutes

to summarize the previous session. Very few professors did this. It was in Dr. Grant's class that I met the beguiling young lady whom I courted for two years prior to going off to Florence. During my year in Italy she was my muse and it was partly to impress her that I tried to make my year abroad as rich as possible in interesting experiences. She typed up many extracts from my letters and circulated them to various professors: Grant, Steinberg, Weinberg, Giese, Andison, etc.

10   (p. 47) Thinking about Canada in 2017 I have a fuller appreciation. It is a relatively compassionate country. Its health care system and most of its universities are excellent.

11   (p. 48) A famous book set in borgo San Frediano is Vasco Pratolini's *Le Ragazze di San Frediano*.

12   (p. 52) Leonard's remark about Canadians being dull and without illusions infuriated me. I had very thin skin in those days and tended to take generalizations as personal affronts. I now think that his remark was quite perceptive.

13   (p. 56) My interest in libretti has been constant throughout my life and led to my writing two books on the subject: *Italian for the Opera* (1991) and *Operatic Italian* (2009). For details see my website: www.godwinbooks.com and my blog, lovesongsinspanish.wordpress.com

14   (p. 58) This first exposure to the subject of Nazi brutality in Italy led to further investigation on my part. I discovered places in Rome which tourists can visit to get a good idea of the brutality and terror of the

German occupation (September 1943 to June 1944): the Gestapo interrogation center on Tasso Street (a few blocks west of the Lateran), which is one of the main scenes in *Roma, Città Aperta* and the Ardeatine Caves located a few miles south of Rome, just west of the Appian Way. These caves witnessed the mass execution of a few hundred innocent Italians as a reprisal for an anti-German act by terrorists. They were tied up and shot and then the caves were dynamited shut. During my visit to these caves I was given a private tour by a Jewish man whose father was one of the victims. These are grim places but I think it is important to know about them. Dante's Ulysses is right: to understand mankind one must know good and evil *"i vizi umani e i valori."*

15   (p. 62) I cringe when I read my political views in 1960. Generally I did not keep well informed about current events. Events later in the 1960s (the death of the Kennedy brothers and Martin Luther King, the Chicago riots, Kent State, and above all, the Vietnam War) appalled me and compelled me to become more aware of politics.

16   (p. 73) George Woodcock (1912-1995) The University of British Columbia almost never hired professors without degrees but in Woodcock's case they made an exception because he had written many brilliant books and was well known in British academic circles (George Orwell was a close friend.) His course on European literature in translation was highly esteemed by students.

17   (p. 76) When I look back on my youth it is clear that at school we had very little training in morality, the virtues and the vices. I doubt if we were even aware of negative things like pride, envy, ire, treachery, or positive things like kindness, compassion, humility, modesty, self-control, etc. When I was in grade eight The British Columbia Department of Education stopped the reading of Bible passages over the school's public address system. I remember thinking it was a shame because I enjoyed the sheer beauty and grandeur of the language. Throughout the rest of my school years I can recall almost no discussion of moral values (although it couldn't be avoided when I encountered Shakespeare's *Julius Caesar, Romeo and Juliet* and *Macbeth*.) Worse, (for me at least) I can recall almost no such discussion in my family of origin. We were stuck in a mute, inarticulate, valueless little world. Going to Florence and reading what Dante has to say about the seven deadly sins was a wonderful revelation. My eyes were opened. Finally, here were the concepts vital to understanding my life and finding a pathway out of the *selva oscura*. It was something I had been thirsting after for years.

18   (p. 79) Vittorio Gassman recites Dante with great sensitivity and power. I have never heard a better reading. In our own time another famous Italian actor, Roberto Benigni, has carried on the Gassman tradition by giving frequent public readings of *La Divina Commedia*. He too reads well. Although he likes to play the clown, when he reads Dante he is very serious and respectful. I have yet to meet an Italian who did

not revere "Padre Dante". Google "oral readings from Dante's *Inferno*" or "Vittorio Gassman reads Dante" and you are in for a treat. Three years after my year in Florence I was in my second year of graduate studies at Yale. Professor T. Bergin asked me to read the Ulysses passage from Dante. I slammed my book shut and theatrically declaimed all twenty-six verses in the original Italian. It might have been impressive but I did not endear myself to my peers who were watching. Damned show off!

19   (p. 92) I think I can speak for my generation of left wing university students when I say that we were very naive in thinking that matters such as "decadence" and "pornography" were without serious inherent dangers. They were very dangerous indeed, as psychologists were to discover (in the 1980s) when they identified 'sexual addictions' and analyzed the havoc they (and pornography) wrought in the lives of many people.

20   (p. 94) Rick wasn't the only North American who wanted to become an Italian. In the movie *Breaking Away* (1979) Dennis Christopher plays a young university student in Indiana who is obsessed with bicycle racing and becoming Italianate.

21   (p.98) The White Spot is a drive-in restaurant chain in Vancouver. They were prized locally for their excellent hamburgers. I car-hopped to help pay my way to university.

22   (p.106) My local library (in Victoria, B.C.) has purchased several Italian television series which center on a police inspector. Watching them gives a good idea

of life in Italy; it is also an excellent way to improve one's understanding of spoken Italian. Three of the best ones are *Commissario Nardone* (set in post World War II Milan), *Commissario Montalbano* (based in Sicily and inspired by Andrea Camilleri's novel), *Commissario Soneri* (*Nebbie e delitti* or *Fogs and crimes*), set in Ferrara.

23   (p.112) I had a big thrill when I visited Venice in the summer of 2015 with copies of my recently printed *Operatic Italian* and found several Venetians (including a lady who sold tickets at the La Fenice Opera House) who were impressed with it and lost no time in buying a copy. For details of the book see my site: www.godwinbooks.com

24   (p. 121) I decided to use in this book many photos from *Il Paesaggio Italico*. Its stark black and white photos from pre-World War One tone in well with the time frame of my stay (1960-61). I have used them for Perugia, Urbino, Assisi, Pisa, Siena, Rome and several other cities.

25   (p. 124) This was a chilling harbinger of things to come. Only six years after I wrote these letters the Arno unleashed its fury on Florence. Dante probably would have exulted in this and seen it as just punishment for the city's iniquities. For those interested in the flood and a panorama of Italian history from 1960 to about 1990 be sure to see *La Meglio Gioventù* (The Best of Our Young People). This movie follows the experiences of two Roman brothers, one a police officer and the other a social worker. For those who love Italy it is obligatory reading.

The terrible flood of November, 1966

Another photo of the flood

Florence, Dante and Me

26   (p. 131) I will feel very gratified if anyone reading this book finds my remarks on families useful. One very important concept is 'family scripts' i.e. certain behaviors and attitudes that are transmitted, often unawares, from generation to generation. Gino's family's love for their mother was a wake-up call for me and got me thinking about my own family scripts, especially lack of love between mother and daughter (and son) and acute sibling rivalry. When my grandmother was widowed, old and frail, my mother refused to take her in to live with us and had her placed in a second rate nursing home. This was part of mother's revenge for my grandmother's siding with my violence-prone biological father and supporting him during my mother's divorce proceedings against him (1946). My mother never forgave my grandmother for doing this and got even. Mother also never forgave her violent ex-husband for abusing her (Serious abuse: punches, black eyes, whippings with a policeman's belt, etc.) and for many years after the divorce she harbored bitterness, a bitterness which spilled over onto me and my brother in the form of emotional detachment and neglect (in her eyes we resembled him a lot). I was too young to understand this (and I'll bet my mother wasn't even aware of it) but I reacted instinctively by walling myself off from her, getting my own revenge by giving her the silent treatment. I too learned to be cruel. Mother retaliated by withdrawing from me even more. Our mutual silence lasted for years and precluded any insight as to what was

happening. The script had worked its way down the line: my grandmother did not support my mother; my mother did not help me in any of the crises of my childhood. Did my retaliation against her for neglecting me and alientating me from my biological father take the form of seeking a new identity that would exclude her: that of an Italian? I think this is quite possible. Another script in our family was acute, physically violent sibling rivalry. (I mention this in my letter of December 4, 1960 in connection with Visconti's *Rocco e i suoi fratelli*.) This rivalry existed between my older brother and me and, in an earlier generation, between my biological father and his younger brother. (The former trapped the latter under a steel tub then sat on it and kept him there all afternoon on a hot summer day.) I only became aware of psychology around 1965 but I realize now that the process of understanding and healing probably started in Torre when I observed the love that Gino's family had for their mother. Living abroad for a year enabled me to see things from a new perspective.

27   (p. 133) Around 1966 I visited Sainte Anne de Beaupré which is just outside of Quebec City. The inner walls of this church are festooned with many discarded crutches. I was impressed and found it impossible not to believe in miracles.

28   (p. 137) On the subject of crime in modern-day Naples I recommend an excellent movie: *Ciao, Professore*. An elementary school teacher from Northern Italy falls victim to a bureaucratic error and is assigned to teach

in a tough suburb of Naples. He soon finds out about the local drug and crime problems.

29 (p. 144) As I look back on things I think I sensed that my muse back in Vancouver might have found a new love interest and that that might account for her long silences. My hunch turned out to be accurate. I was in no position to feel self-righteous, however, because I had met a Florentine chemistry student, Laura C., who cast a spell on me. She had that special Botticelli blonde look—a mixture of spirituality and refined sensuality—that you can spot sometimes in Florence (I have seen such faces in shop girls in downtown Florence.) She had a sweet, even-tempered personality and the gift of making a man feel enfolded and validated. I went with her to a few Sunday afternoon dances at Fiesole and at the Student Union. My conversational Italian took a huge leap forward when I started spending time with her. Some lovely little details I recall: dancing close to what were to me very romantic new songs like Mina's *Cielo in una stanza* (Try googling it.) and Peppino di Capri's *Luna Caprese*; her stroking the back of my hand and commenting on the protruding veins: *Suggeriscono la forza. (They suggest strength)* she said, smiling and gazing into my eyes. What a lovely thing to hear a woman say! Such subtle recognition of one's masculinity. She broke things off after about a month but did it with real kindness and style, giving me as a farewell keepsake a pair of gold cuff-links with the Florentine lily engraved on them. The lady in Vancouver was told nothing of this little interlude although it's possible she suspected something.

30   (p. 145) James Inkster. I recall Mr. Inkster announcing over the public address system that *Rigoletto* would be shown on television over the weekend and that it was well worth watching. After he made that announcement he could do no wrong in my eyes! I should add that Mr. Inkster dared to talk about values. To link back with footnote 17 I still recall his excellent talk on the damaging effects of malicious gossip among students.

31   (p. 145) In the movie *The Amazing Mr. Ripley*, Matt Damon gets fitted by an Italian tailor and orders some suits. This scene brings back to me my visits to Signor Annichini and I have watched it more times than I care to admit. How thrilling, to order one's first suit!

32   (p.160) If I could do the year over I would buy a scooter as soon as possible. It would save a great deal of time and exploring the country would be so much easier. I would also advise anyone embarking on a year abroad program to beware of trying to save money by settling for cheap but depressing accommodation. Keeping one's morale up is important. So is fitness. I let my fitness level slide and put on some fat. Not good! Joining a fitness club would be a smart idea.

33   (p.192) The special charm of Capri sets the stage for one of Somerset Maugham's best short stories, *The Lotus Eaters*.

34   (p. 208) I returned to Vancouver in late June and within a few days the lady I wrote the letters to stepped out of my life. It was a major blow, I have to say. That summer (1961) I took two upper division courses at the University of British Columbia and studied with a vengeance. I had the great good fortune to study with two very remarkable teachers who just happened to be teaching there for the summer. One was Dr. Daniel Poirion (of Yale University) who gave a brilliant survey course on seventeenth century French literature. The other was Dr. Jean Darbelnet (of Laval University) who gave a course on the twentieth century novel in France. Darbelnet had written a brilliant book, *Stylistique comparé du français et de l'anglais*, which shows in depth how at an unconscious 'metalinguistic' level English and French differ in their essence (e.g. French tends to favor the abstract, English the concrete.) and that translators must take this into account when they translate. During the next academic year (1961-2) I finished my honors B.A. degree at UBC and was awarded a Woodrow Wilson fellowship which paid most of my expenses towards a PhD from Yale in Romance languages (1966). The things I learned during my year in Florence stood me in good stead throughout these years of study and for many years afterwards.

35   (p. 210) David Trott became a great friend and colleague. He went on to the University of Toronto, got his PhD there and had long, distinguished career as a professor at the Erindale branch of that university.

He passed away in 2006 and had a theater named in his honor at the Erindale campus.

36   (p. 212) I returned to Florence several times over the years. During my visit there in 1994 I went around to Ede Parenti's place in Via dei Serragli. Alas, she and Colonel Cugiani had long since died. It seemed that everything had changed: the friendly bookseller's stall was gone, there was no trace of the *vinaio* or the communal showers. Italia's *trattoria* was no longer there. I buzzed myself into the landing at the bottom of the stairs to Ede's place and called out her name a few times. No answer but in my mind I could hear very distinctly her voice saying "Chi è?" (Who's there?). I felt a lump in my throat, my eyes misted up, and I left.

37   (p. 215) *son et lumière:* an entertainment held by night at a historic monument or building, telling its history by the use of recorded sound and lighting effects.

Photo Credits

I acknowledge with gratitude permission to use photos from:

1. Alinari, Vittorio. *Il paesaggio italico nella Divina Comme-dia*. Florence: G. and P. Alinari, 1921

   > Perugia (p. 6), Assisi (p. 8), Urbino (p. 13), Pisa (p. 68), Mantua (p. 109), La rupe tarpea in Rome (p. 141), Siena (p. 177). The page references refer to the text of *Florence, Dante and Me*.

2. *Italy at War:* one volume in a set of 32 volumes found in the collection World War II. Alexandria, VA: Time-Life Books, 1982.

   > Italian partisans fighting in Florence (p. 56), Italians seized at random and led to their execution (p. 58), war ruins of Milan (p. 69). The page references refer to the text of *Florence, Dante and Me*.

About the Author

Robert Thomson was born in Vancouver in 1940. He graduated from West Vancouver High School in 1958 then went to the University of British Columbia where he graduated in 1962 with a first class honors degree in French and Italian. While doing his B.A. Thomson was awarded a one year scholarship to attend the University of Florence; he also received a Woodrow Wilson fellowship (1962) which he used to attend Yale University. He received his PhD from Yale in 1966. (Thomson says that one of his biggest thrills in life was to see two much-admired people on the same stage as himself: Barbara Tuchman and "Duke" Ellington.) After a teaching career Thomson took early retirement (1995) and set up his own publishing house, Godwin Books. **(www.godwinbooks.com)** He has published several of his own books and has been instrumental in reprinting and gaining recognition for the books of his great-uncle, George Godwin (1889-1974).

Other Books by
Robert Stuart Thomson

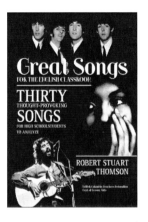

Great Songs for the English Classroom (1980). Thirty thought-provoking songs for high school stúdents to analyze. Students listen to the songs and print the missing words on cloze outlines. This is followed by a class discussion and journal writing. Working on songs develops listening skills, provides a review of basics (spelling, vocabulary) and offers the student a forum in which to explore important issues such as love, friendship, peer pressure, parental neglect, alienation, and anger. This book was published by the British Columbia Teachers Federation Dept. of Lesson Aids.

Italian for the Opera (1991). 150 pages, with black and white photos. Examines in depth many extracts from operas and discusses subtleties such as connotation, layers of meaning, and aspects of the composer which surface in the text. At the same time it analyses in logical order parts of speech. Includes quizzes to monitor progress plus an index. This book sold out in 2003 after an initial print run of 2000 and has recently (2013) been reprinted.

Operatic Italian (2009). 460 pages, with many photos and IPA used throughout. A huge expansion of "Italian for the Opera", this book contains several new chapters: how to study operatic Italian on your own, the sounds and rhythm of Italian, suitable esthetic criteria for judging operatic Italian, what to read for good plot outlines, the pros and cons of subtitles, the influence of Dante, operatic language in canzoni, a brief look at Neapolitan. "*Operatic Italian* would make a fantastic textbook for a conservatory or university." – Sarah Luebke, *Opera Today*, 2010.

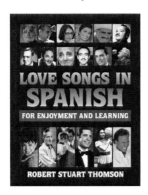

Love Songs in Spanish (2016). This 125 page book contains 24 outstanding love songs in the Spanish language. They cover a wide range of genres, recording artists and countries. The book comes with a free CD. Listening to songs and studying them is one of the best ways to acquire good pronunciation and an appreciation of the inherent musicality of Spanish. You also learn new vocabulary, idioms, and grammar points. Last but not least, "Love Songs in Spanish" gives you cultural insight. Each song comes with a reliable Spanish version, an accurate translation (using the interlinear format as much as possible), language notes and information on composers, lyricists and recording artists. See *Hispania*, Dec.2016

All of these books can be seen and ordered
on my website:
www.godwinbooks.com

My blog:
www.lovesongsinspanish.wordpress.com

You will find on my site the table of contents,
sample passages from the books, and reviews by critics.
Order these books – paperback or eBook –
online or mail your cheque to Robert Thomson:
PO Box 50021, Victoria, B.C.
Canada V8S 5L8.